DIMESTORE SAINTS

Dimestore Saints

SONNETS
from the
GOSPEL OF ST. MATTHEW

DAVID CRAIG

Copyright © David Craig 2025
Waterloo, ON N2J 0A5
www.aroucapress.com

All rights reserved.
No part of this book may be reproduced or transmitted, in any form or by any means, without permission.

ISBN: 978-1-998492-29-9 (pbk)
ISBN: 978-1-998492-30-5 (hc)

Contents

The Large and the Small   1
The Holy Family   2
FOR THE TIME BEING   3
It's Never a Good Idea to Kill a Baby   4
Madonna House Artists   5
The Desert Call   6
Mercy's Tool   7
First Eucharist   8
Men Fast to Burn Away Their Appetites   9
It could have been in St. Peter's Square   10
It's not Much, I Know   11
Where People Sit in Darkness   12
The Price   13
Who can Hear This?   14
For Fr. Pelton, Madonna House Spiritual Director   15
On Thérèse's Knee   16
Blessed are the Peacemakers   17
Careers   18
Ants Raise Two Arms   19
Fool's Gold   20
Up the Rockies to Grad School   21
Yes and No   22
After Scott Cairns's "On Slow Learning"   23
Forget the Law and Live It   24
The Lion, the Witch …   25
The Violence of God   26
For Fr. Callahan, Madonna House Priest   27
For Billy Holiday   28
St. Catherine of Siena's would-be Paramour   29
The World is Thy Ship and not Thy Home   30
Feed Your Cares to Twain   31
Walter Mitty, Crowding   32
Pearls before Swine   33

The Other World 34
Gamaliel's Rule 35
The Narrow Gate 36
Catherine Doherty 37
"I Never Knew You" 38
Houses Built on Rock 39
Winning My Leprosy 40
A Man under Authority 41
Mothers-in-Law 42
Judgment 43
Wherever You Go 44
What can You Say to the Sea? 45
On a Theme Lifted from C. S. Lewis 46
Jesus Blasphemes 47
Matthew, in the Counting House 48
Matthew, with Sinners 49
New Wineskins 50
Keener 51
Mary's Eyes 52
"He Casts Out Demons..." 53
Bound by Two Hands 54
No One Else has ever Spoken Like This 55
Saints are Never Sure 56
Do not Fear 57
Bad (Older) Parents 58
No Father 59
The Clown's Red Nose 60
Feasting with Fallen Women 61
"To What shall I Liken this Generation?" 62
So, You're Saying there's a Chance? 63
For Jude, at 10 64
As Supple as Grain 65
Alphonse Liguori's Meditations on Death 66
In His Name the Gentiles will Trust 67
Catherine's Clemency 68
By Its Fruit 69

In the Eyes of Men   70
This World We Live In   71
Mary's Moon   72
The Whole Came First   73
Madonna House, Walmart, and Stevens   74
Where Colored Doors Can Close   75
"Parker's Back"   76
Mustard Plants   77
The Holy Hand Grenade   78
Down Time   79
St. Pio's Pearl   80
Jesus's New Earring   81
On the Rooftops with Handel   82
His Lizard Hands   83
Hell in Ringlets   84
What John had Planted   85
"To Make an End…"   86
When the King Appears   87
Hippy Law   88
Waiting Loudly (in Glasgow)   89
The Truth must Shock Us Blind   90
Parents   91
What We're Made For   92
The Rest of the News   93
When Signs Ask for One   94
The Multiplication   95
The Son of the Living God   96
Our Notion, Our Fuss   97
The Help We Get   98
The Book of Him   99
Elijah   100
Happy Dis   101
The Lies at the Local Library   102
Peter Fishes   103
He Talked to Me   104
An End We'll All Face   105

The Delayed should be Allowed 106
Three Stories 107
Chicka Chicka Boom Boom 108
Bosnia-Herzegovina 109
At the Carnival 110
Play 111
The Rose at Hand 112
Old House 113
These Popes 114
Leaving Room 115
The Time for Great Deeds 116
Thy Brothers' Elbows 117
For Yeats 118
Keaton and Chaplin 119
Donkeys Belong 120
Children Take the Temple Floor 121
Dressed in Blue 122
DRY SALVAGES 123
Harlots Who Go on Speaking 124
O'Connor, Shouting 125
Pay Whatever is Due 126
Talkers 127
The Sadducees 128
A Corpse's Flowered Jaw 129
Nothing Comes Next 130
Miserere 131
The Sevenfold Indictment 132
The Untroubled Hand 133
70 AD 134
The Devil Ages 135
"Whoever Reads…" 136
Wherever the Carcass Is 137
The Last Symphony 138
Even in Heaven 139
Late Test 140
In the Shack, Left Behind 141

Irenaeus and Gnosis   142
God as a Mellon   143
Lukewarm, or Just Middling   144
A One Man Show   145
Beauty is Where It Finds You   146
A Man of Dice   147
Miracles   148
Clay Houses   149
The First Tree   150
Peter's Pence   151
Gethsemani   152
The Kiss   153
Can't Get There from Here   154
The Best Sit Somewhere Else   155
The Chief (and Lesser) Priests   156
Each Balanced Thing   157
The King of the Jews   158
There is a Silence   159
Then they Crucified Him   160
The Louder We Talk   161
The Dead Out Walking   162
Every Day under Sun   163
A Pagan Pilate   164
"Your Sweet Wife/Will Catch More Fish than You"   165
"Rejoice!"   166
Our Elders   167
The Riotous Good   168

About the Author   169

The Large and the Small
(MATTHEW 1:1-17)

God's book sounds sunny oceans, the Maccabees.
We swirl in ancient winds, hear our glyphs, names,
snaking in sand; shaded in stenciled trees—
our ancestry. The planet is His loving, maimed.
(Our brain pans control a rolling, circular pea.
We work out the math, then call the process our own.)
This book insists on the One who turns each leaf,
who's large enough to play this pile of bones!
He would have us love each other, pick up the poor,
the rich, respect each name. He writes out time,
giving folks floor enough to freely explore
their dance. He takes each symbol, makes it a sign.
From the Self that's Heaven, Heaven becomes the Man
who speaks every tongue, offers a completing hand.

The Holy Family
(MATTHEW 1:18–25)

Her days passed in breezes, palm trees at noon,
the granular water jar as it scraped along
the top of the well. This world, though scarred, was a boon,
unclaimed, because people couldn't hear love's song
give rise to the law, the Heart that would restore
the lost, that would coax the people's spirits to flame:
"Messiah." She could hear that rising whisper, bore
Him close — though whose heart could carry that name!
And as for everyman Joseph? He walked the laws' lines,
what he knew of freedom. Yes, He'd seen priests stretch
the scrolls pretty thin. For greed (perhaps), these signs
which led him. So he built himself with carpentry tools.
As husbands, wives did, they kept their daily pace.
Through grace and absence, He showed His human face.

FOR THE TIME BEING
(MATTHEW 2:1-12)

The teachers of the law, the privileged priests,
he knew, found ease in parchment: "These foreigners chase
the hatted seed!" So Herod fumed, left his feast—
to put on Auden's tiresome civic face:
"Oh Bethlehem, what have you done to my profits?"
(He knew the cold, but without winter's expanse,
he had no way of feeling his way, its fit—
Holy poverty's clubfoot, its Christmas dance.)
And the better kings? They camelled along, "overjoyed,"
humping over mounds of sand—though Eliot's death
would close behind like the consolation it buoyed:
that life only comes with boyhood's restless breath.
Wisdom and childhood dance in a snowy wood,
where midnight sparkles, and something is understood.

It's Never a Good Idea to Kill a Baby
(MATTHEW 2:13-20)

Evil must have its day, that's how we know
that life is real, and why each story matters.
Evil keeps us from seeing Christmas as glistening bows.
It walks down happy Main, Herod's dark hatter.
He can shine, on the finest avenues: New York shops,
salons, in the homes of the poor. He gets his stay;
though he's pure negation, is offered no chair. (He stops
nothing!) Evil's how we learn courage — to faithfully stray.
What he steals slips through his fingers, his ancient moan.
He works the darkness, inventing histories,
killing for loss — while dead babe and forgotten crone
move on and away. (They never pass the same tree!)
Babies have always set us free, cheeks round
as apples; they steal our hearts — and we're found, crowned.

Madonna House Artists
(MATTHEW 2:21-23)

In Nazareth, the drudgery of rote
is unlearned: we find our way through chores, in friends.
Each sacrifice made, each small cross borne is a mote
of testimony which tells us — what could offend
more than hesitant hands? So let joy reveal
Himself as He will then. We will learn as we must,
praising in hidden days, cranking a wheel
by an opened window, where, as gladsome dust,
we ply our trades, weave each alleluia
to sighs, trading our time for a place; the shapes,
a quiet junket of kazoos and pennants because
we can: miming God in a swirl of capes.
In art we take His hands, each moment's loss,
and find the joy in our waiting: Pentecost.

The Desert Call
(MATTHEW 3:1-6)

Wisdom walks in the desert, has legs like an insect.
You quiet to try and hear the chirring, take in
the pincers, the scraping—learn. But he doesn't beck
to your call. (You will do the traveling, Sin.)
Pharisees speak in every sect, though wisdom
always walks alone. We try to follow, in Judea
tonight—its buses, bars (in pipes, Scotch drums).
You'll fit in as well as John: without any idea.
Come with your life in your hands, a victim of
your petty distress. You'll learn to sit among weeds.
Absence is the grace you need. You'll find love
there, as your knowledge, sense of self falls to seed.
Jesus, let me go his way, a peaceful waif.
A place where I can and can't be kept quiet, safe.

Mercy's Tool
(MATTHEW 3:7-12)

This brood of vipers, fleeing their coming fall,
are torn between the need they own, and the fee
they charge to get there. They wear their colors for all
to see, these would-be limbs on Abraham's tree.
But John is the desert talking, won't give them rain.
He offers repentance — speech they've never heard.
(There can be no favor for the sons of Cain,
only the demands of the Torah, its embodied Word,
because Mercy never changes. It gives us the rod
we are — our wheat and chaff, this mortal mire.)
One dare not mimic the holiness of God!
The winnowing fan spreads both love and ire.
Mercy's tool, Justice, can almost walk alone.
Its limp defines us: our hunger, our search for home.

First Eucharist
(MATTHEW 3:13-17)

To raise the earth to sacrament he ties
Himself to the lowest face. And from John's place,
the Servant, rising, scatters the wealthy, the wise,
gives each disciple bread, an unleavened face.
(Did John at that moment see the Temple rend?
Did he see this Man, our God, eclipsing death,
come back, as the lit-up shroud found a way to descend —
men later eating that Body, breathing that Breath?)
Did he see the water part, Christ's arms on His chest,
when the Father spoke, created the priestly paten:
"Here dies the rest of the poor," all wrongs redressed
in the love of God, in the brokenness that brings?
We need to be lifted up: our goods, our friends,
our sense of who's poor, the need for a worthy end.

Men Fast to Burn Away Their Appetites
(MATTHEW 4:1-4)

"Men fast to burn away their appetites,
to make You the pristine centerpiece of their lives,
to move the locus of need one inch to the right.
They deny themselves, and hope, in death, to survive.
But why do You fast? To try on hunger's need,
to take man's bridle, to mouth his tired bit?
Will You become Your own dark night, will You feed
on the loss so You almost know the faith of it?
Get real. Affirm matter, which from hope sprung.
That's why You came, isn't it? To make everything a sign.
So do like she'll tell You. What's a few stones among
friends? Bread or wine, it all gets left behind.
In what jail house is this truth I speak a crime?"

"Oh taste and see.... The law is food Divine!"

It could have been in St. Peter's Square
(MATTHEW 4:5–7)

"It could have been in St. Peter's Square, a lousy
Pope on either wing. Or perhaps in Mecca,
in later days, believers, by then, too drowsy
to sing: whom He was sent for, trying to check
Him. The same old devils, bringing what they bring:
'We know Your Name; we know what You will do:
defeat the elements, flay Yourself—a King!
You atone for Your plan.... Please do, generous ewe.
Your bleating fouls the stage You've made! And Your law?
A sham! Go ahead—take a real chance; the streets,
the angels will save you! Even now I would offer a paw
to protect my Maker, part of creation, sweet.'"

"Vision is a canker to those who think to see.
As gods they narrow, yet never cease to be."

It's not Much, I Know
(MATTHEW 4:8-11)

"It's not much, I know, what with slums and the
    dubious types
who sit at the better tables. Still, one can whine
forever, can't one? Take what comes when it's ripe,
I say. Pleasure's not an evil if taken as a sign
that life is good. There is an ease one can find
in this place: the limited joys that come with largesse.
I've come to like it, a shock, perhaps from a mind
once filled with higher saws. Welcome… to 'The Best
We Can Do.' Allow me to pour you a middling sherry.
The decanter is chipped, but the maids here are lively,
    can laugh.
And, if you'll allow, performers will keep us merry.
I'll call for a tweedler, one who knows his craft."

"You serve yourself at table, eat your tail.
My lovers reach, even now, for the wood, for the nails."

Where People Sit in Darkness
(MATHEW 4:12-17)

It's a dark mimesis, Death. Seeing, he prods
with what seems a foot. He asks for the Baptist, makes
him John the less too soon, this mime of God,
trumped spade! He imitates sleep, but never wakes.
Look: as shadow he brings the Man, a band
of funny Galileans, and more of the lost
in Capernaum by the sea (having built on sand).
Who else but God would choose such layered dross?
May our sins, like Naphtali's, start to fall by degrees—
though we Jungian shadows by death, unclench our wills
so slowly you'd think death charged a shopping fee!
(What is night, sin, when they die on each southern sill?)
Darkness is a shade. His song is not his own.
He takes the sun's, leaves it singing to bones.

The Price
(MATTHEW 4:18–22)

What was it that drew Him? Andrew and Simon, their
   backs
working the present, intense in their fish through strife;
not ambitious, but fierce as they now changed course,
   attacked
His bait: their song, for the nets of eternal life.
And then the apposite pair: more thoughtful, John
and James, mending (many) nets, under their patriarch.
They were the not-quite-ready, hurried along
by the Hand who knows when to pluck: Mercy's lark,
beyond good sense. And then Zebedee, in the boat;
not alone, but rocking in a father's sorrow. His sons,
gone in the heaven that takes us all. Nets afloat,
he now lived in love; "Messiah" had begun.
Any man would follow, or give his sons in his stead.
He'd walk with God, add grief to his dying bed.

Who can Hear This?
(MATTHEW 4:23-25)

Who can hear this? He boldly proclaimed Himself
as the answer; not indirectly as most do, but boldly
and in works; the littered sin, our garden's pelf,
no longer rejected, but raised with ease from the moulds,
as amid excited screams, disturbed wonder,
even the dead were given life at His breath,
His word. And this Law they thought they knew, sundered
by a youth who'd loose the phylacteries of death.
From ten towns, barren rabbis, the hungry came,
and then into synagogues where He spoke like no
one else had, the Torah. The learned, first drawn by
    His fame,
hung slack-jawed, fed by the harvest they'd labored to sow.
His speech, which He is, offers us life, our God.
But then He's gone, and we're left with absence: His rod.

For Fr. Pelton, Madonna House Spiritual Director
(MATTHEW 5:1-5)

The poor in spirit don't own their shirt, or their back.
They live downtown, might have a little dog.
Their music comes from a plastic radio, a stack
of LPs. They eat in soup kitchens — adjust in fog.
No one knows if they're guests or community workers.
Blessed are those who mourn. What else could they do?
They are poustinikis (or Communists). Or shirkers,
though how they're perceived only matters in
    Saturday's pew.
Blessed are the meek. They alone will stock the earth.
They'll play cards by the old kitchen wood-burning stove.
(Maybe you've seen them on some other turf.
They move through lots of places. They were meant to
    rove.)
Jesus, maker of ways; complete what you start.
I waste in shallow sins, a satisfied heart.

On Thérèse's Knee
(MATTHEW 5:6-8)

Happy the child who seeks a righteousness
he can't control. He knows his empty place
by the crosses, which always come in local dress:
the graces he can't draw, but needs to trace.
Happy, his home is on Thérèse's knee,
a bearded fool Mercy wounds—tears big as peonies.
He sounds the child, wanting his father's squeeze,
expressing his exasperation with a "Pl-e-ease. . . !"
Happy and pure, he likes his jazz wafer thin;
he rides the cool as it mutes and works the noise,
Miles Davis at a bar, that introspective din.
(Let me clatter my piety, scat our mutual joy!)
Walking with saints and angels, the sweat of praise,
let me toast my Jesus, disrupt harmonious days.

Blessed are the Peacemakers
(MATTHEW 5:9-12)

Blessed are those who've endured the passing boots,
who've seen each film, who've paged through the lore
   of battle—
Zeppelin field; the stolen paintings, all the loot;
who've watched the Gestapo herd Jews like cattle.
The persecuted, as well, know the dream of home,
the life they cannot have—what liars can't see.
They spend their time in the quiet, restless, alone;
they are as natural as rain, following seed.
Blessed are the slurred who gather us in.
Their world's remade in every generation.
They sound our woe, as He opens His arms to sin.
They look for enemies and find they have none!
They might be the prophets' footstools, their shoulders,
   rests.
Gerasim could call them "Tolstoy," "Little guests."

Careers
(MATTHEW 5:13-16)

The man who strives past station is left with none.
He must be overlooked, or he is a spice
without a table, but nothing else: a run
at what is, missing the seasons, as homey as rice.
So let the salted shine, like a hilltop lamp,
like nothing else in Galilee. Let them sing
their children's songs, stockings, soiled and damp
by the door, days which only the days can bring.
(Salt over my left shoulder, not over my right!)
No! Let the alleys know us, five, as we sing.
Tambourines and puppies, popcorn late at night.
May our kids know porch glory, a crowded swing.
Salt belongs to the earth (though lore knows better).
It finds place on the table, a spirit that spells the letter.

Ants Raise Two Arms
(MATTHEW 5:17-19)

The law's a magic blanket, blinking stars.
You wear it around your shoulders, find it warms
the coldest night. It coaxes fire. The far
ends of evening follow suit, offer their form.
The Pharisees had to know this, the One whose ease
created them. Love needs no other way.
(And what is law except the leaves on a tree?
On its limbs, upside down, the grace of God sways.)
His mercy is the day: the process, the whole.
We seek His heart, get dappled by what is true.
And so your blanket shines at night. (It's the role
your sins have played.) Ants raise two arms on cue!
Who would we be if everything came out skewed?
Michelangelo sculpted, the rest of us hew.

Fool's Gold
(MATTHEW 5:20-26)

The slap of water should be enough. Otters,
swimming alongside, vying with spray, some hiss.
It could be a nautical life of sons and daughters.
Such should be the extent of our foolishness —
since this is a place for diminishing returns.
Your gift was grandly expected, friend; it's made you
an amenable, error-proned neighbor. Don't the ferns
turn his head as well? (Allow him the larger hue
and cry!) Raca's your middle name. Leave the altar
to the holy, settle your claims, and friends — if possible.
Who wants to pay a hefty fare and then falter,
take half a peach basket when you could have a full?
Teach me the silence, Lord, of all-outdoors.
Let me sift through nature, bless what trout are for.

Up the Rockies to Grad School
(MATTHEW 5:27-32)
—*AKITA, JAPAN*

The sin right at your doorstep, or over someone
else's; the custody required when the eye
is only a look away. Think of that nun,
or our Mother, who quietly suffers each passing lie.
And though it's hard to imagine one so meek
crushing a head, she knows the depths of this world,
people cut off from the "yes" He gave her to speak.
She offers her eyes like Oedipus. (Jellied pearls!)
We breathe most freely at the river's source.
Range and the dependent self will start to crack,
fissures gape, and a mountainous April course
of flood will bristle, convex, like our only way back.
Our sins always long to take up more space than they need.
They would define us, stand in a breech and feed.

Yes and No
(MATTHEW 5:33–37)

Our Mother, Teresa, lived her life like this,
her "Yes," larger than speech. But we saw and were called
by what she would also say, this world's abbess,
loving Calcutta because it was the fall.
"No" was absence, so she took no note. There were
the dying to wash, the dead with TVs, alone
in their prosperity, that hackled cur
who dogs our money as if it were spiritual bone.
Losing judgment, her mind became a place
for angels, her affirmation, a door for the poor.
In her we saw our God's Albanian face.
We could stable there, in the Wounded Heart she bore.
Self-consciousness had no place in her daily rounds.
She needed Jesus to be both fore and ground.

After Scott Cairns's "On Slow Learning"
(MATTHEW 5:38–42)

We are the knights of imagined slights. It's like Twain
said, most tragedies never happen. We're laid bare
by each contrary soul we meet, each permitted pain
we bear, because we don't see the faces God wears.
"If you counter ideas, don't counter the man you see.
He is God's word," Kirshna, armed, might tell us.
"Don't resist the man or his humanity. . . .
But kill without passion because you too are dust."
Poets are the yeses I walk on, their turning cheeks,
each's only way. I drink from Jacob's well,
til I'm robbed of place, in front of the almost-meek,
and then I stand, convicted by what I sell.

Generosity comes, a turtle, almost walking in place.
Give him a break. . . . He doesn't manufacture grace!

Forget the Law and Live It
(MATTHEW 5:43-48)

Forget the law and live it, or, better, run
for joy because you can. "Godly ways" will fade
like the morning's respectable air. Clouds or sun
will shine on a face simplicity has made.
Let the work of holy men rumble past you
with their engines. You have nothing they'd want to steal.
They are you in better clothes. Love them, each new
and manicured landscape, the banes which keep you real.
Talk to Blake beneath his window, share your zeal
with someone who hasn't learned a thing in years,
who loves the quiet and waits for God's Hand to steal
each apparent victory, loss, whatever is dear.
Our spheres of influence grow as our plans recede,
as we claim our stake in the Heart which gives us need.

The Lion, the Witch . . .
(MATTHEW 6:1-6)

The faithful should pray inside a closet of bone.
Each should inspect his hands in the lamplit light,
get used to the flaws, learn to call them home.
How else will we ever hope to get this right?
It's easy to think we'd never advertise or fawn.
After all, we glide on grand sleds over frozen seas.
(But the hairs of self-promotion are counted on
our heads; each speaks of our duplicity.
So where can we find wardrobes furry enough
to find us missing, yet living abundant lives?
How can we forgive completely, carry each cuff,
each angry flaw, our lonely midnight drives?)
We've got to go when we know we can never be true.
To tell the Truth—a terrible thing to do.

The Violence of God
(MATTHEW 6:7–15)

An unnamed pull, imbedded in darkness, reveals
itself in time, a human's angst; God knows
us alive in the rough blood-soil of His peel-
off, a husk of self torn as the seedling now bows,
muscle-bends, giving the greening the time it needs.
We begin once again; the Father creates the prayer
He is, written in every flower, bleeds
in its being, the Eucharist—the only way there.
Only then can we verbalize a daemon need:
the sins we can never seem to shake. His hand
is upon us. He asks for foolish hearts, then leads
us, children, to our plow blade, opening land.
Forgiveness is lush, wide as the Father's heart.
Open it. And its careful soil rips apart.

For Fr. Callahan, Madonna House Priest
(MATTHEW 6:16-18)

We need two faces, a double chin, one pair
of eyes to watch the other wince, to ignore
his fasts, his stamps and whistles, our final glare
as the better us stands guard, a smile at the door.
But our dying half will not want to play, to stay
in the crypt. A guest may recall a trace of moan,
the mission far behind the voice, the way
I remember his almost silent gift, which honed
Him until he died, a living sacrifice
of praise as he carried others' burdens behind
the gravel, the measured words, paying the price
of the cross as he'd talk or fish, a hollowing rind.
This quiet before me, I had to listen to see
how he died to himself in the Masses at Calvary.

For Billy Holiday
(MATTHEW 6:19–21)

To live where our treasure is, where we'd like to be
doesn't sound much like a heroic task.
The blues are better there; the toast, the tea.
But something in us requires revelry, a masque:
the deadened hours perhaps, the two-faced mirror.
We'd die for Southampton's art, Bacon's scope,
more room so we won't see our cabin stir.
We don't want to be found here, victims of a stagnant hope.
But those sloughs of despond can reveal quieter needs,
and who can see what they lack until the winds blow,
until, in bitter snow, we must wait for the seed,
God dancing so slowly, it seems He'll never show?
We all must spend some time, lost on our cross.
A lesser "Strange Fruit," our gift is also our dross.

St. Catherine of Siena's would-be Paramour
(MATTHEW 6:22–23)

His darkened eye distorted to avoid that toad,
life. To see would bruise the ego, to take
his place on a faceless penitential road.
But this other had a self, a niche to make.
And if what was real had to die for him to get
the reaction he wanted, he'd use that loss to beat
his friends, the Fellowship. Feeding on holy regret,
she'd pay for the love he offered, its languished heat.
And they did suffer, because he never quite sensed
the leer behind his grin. In quiet, subdued
Christian letters, written from his personal bench,
he preened a sickness over the people he knew.
Deciding on distance, he'd dangle just out of reach;
a puppet showing his strings, like a day at the beach.

The World is Thy Ship and not Thy Home
(MATTHEW 6:24)

Jesus moves our deepest current. Life's not a star,
a choice here or there, but Being who owns you, a bin
that slowly fills up next to a biker bar.
It's abandonment. He doesn't care about sin!
He cares about the spreading chestnut tree.
He knows virtue is a loping dog, his tongue
alongside. Perfection does Its work—to best
Itself, which is a way of saying we're sung:
Love brings us home. We just have to get a read,
write the next line. "Come with me, little one," is
His refrain. We walk His shore, say His beads—
out over an opal-streaked sea as we stand in the fizz
at our feet. Jesus, let me drift in the creak of my boat.
Hand on gunnel, I'll watch with Thérèse, take notes.

Feed Your Cares to Twain
(MATTHEW 6:25–34)

Feed your cares to the birds; if you make them bread,
they will eat. Otherwise, they will do no good,
either to you or the fiction you walk in. Instead,
let us work in palimpsest: in leisure which stood
by Twain, like Huck, as he rafted, each new river,
a Mississippi; just a pole, calm stars
to wile away the catfish nights, a sliver
of moon, cabin's lantern beyond the bar.
Twain added the tar, of course, the king, the duke.
He made up every day then night of rain.
Leisure's tramp, he tried each puddle, his flukes,
because he saw the world in grandma's lane.
Wear the warm air, lilies will be your staff.
Playful worms will scratch you an epitaph!

Walter Mitty, Crowding
(MATTHEW 7:1-5)

Old habits are tough to break, tickering parades
because who else can come so close to the mind
of God? We're products of youthful barricades:
vanity, our defense against absent parents we pined
for. Even now, I cattle myself, believe
that only a pompous other would fall in a ditch
of his own making. A spiritual Mitty, I'm deceived
by the burden of perfect judgment, my ark's dark pitch.
Prayer's the answer, of course. It's always been.
But how can I deflate complacency
when Walter crowds me on buses, borrowing pens,
passing gossip that begins and ends with me.
Lord, let me count the turnips on my truck.
Let me bump along, without a bit of luck.

Pearls before Swine
(MATTHEW 7:6)

We live in two faces, though one you seldom see;
that world, an invisible oyster, sporting pearls
from no sea. His better kingdom is yet to be;
so we stand erect, try to keep our flagging furled,
for we serve, you see, an exacting, absent Lord,
and though we know we are not worthy to trod
this path, nor can we count the cache we've stored,
we beat the only, the narrow road to God.
It's absurd, materialists say: this nosing the air,
sniffing for scentless clues, pretending our lot
makes us better, pure bred, set apart, like some rare
and bloodless species, they a mutt-like blot.
This "chosen" bit can snag. What can we do?
Limp on, until they see the other shoe.

The Other World
((MATTHEW 7:7-11))

The other world is one of plenty, with ripe
answers for our question which drop from the vine.
It's a world we know, where the throated pipes
of lilies finish each partially scripted line.
It's where we're called, in joy, beyond the "here,"
where what is real seldom happens, as far
as the eye can see. It's where the Answer's so near
you walk It, like wise men calling down the star.
It's madness to live where Jesus is, in the spring
of what's yet fully to be, where the asked-for fast
from sin and food makes stone-hearted Abrahams sing.
Touched by heaven's reach, we exceed our grasp.
To be a fool like the world had never seen:
so Francis was, but the place was always green.

Gamaliel's Rule
(MATTHEW 7:12)

Christ may have lifted this, though He thought of it first,
since every truth emanates from a God
who is love and gives form to this world. Our creative bursts
come out of the earth — its sacramental sod.
Who of us owns a speck of His virtue, could decree
a plan to save us, bit by blessed bit?
When zealot Paul says, "It's Christ who lives in me,"
it's not hyperbole. God has found him fit
for dress. As man, our Paul is dust, like before
his turn — having given the very life he sought!
And this is where we stick: that at our core,
our egos matter so much less than we'd thought.
But in God's sight we are golden, flesh and tooth,
a boast from One who can only speak the truth.

The Narrow Gate
(MATTHEW 7:13-14)

The gate is Confessional thin, more narrow within.
We follow, gracefully awkward. A sign of the cross
marks us; then a priest's insight, outside the din
of the media world, measures what we've lost.
And though a prodigal joy lights up heaven,
here we still hack thin paths, proceed with what passes
for speed, getting correctional glimpses, leaven:
our sorry resolve — one wrong turn, and we're asses
again, sporting our need for the infantile.
Not quite the "narrow" He means! This is where we live,
or where too much of us does. Again we taste bile —
what follows: humility as a kind of sieve!
The road to heaven is heaven, all the saints say;
it's less-travelled on because so much of it strays.

Catherine Doherty
(MATTHEW 7:15–20)

Though Satan might own a pose to hook the sheep,
anti-papal Catholics won't be outdone.
Respected prophetic members, are they part of a deep
wisdom, a book-selling clan who best know the Son?
Or are they gnostics? Look at Versailles, where teas
once portended the end of a world. Tepid prophets
    these days
deride "popesplaining," work parish halls, the rough Sees
of Peter. (If you want prayer, they've counted the ways,)
But heaven can only be found on peasants' knees,
in hovels with broken space heaters, lambs in and out,
their droppings. Somewhere patched—not with
    spiritual brie.
(The poor have more questions than answers; own no
    clout.)
Save us from Catholic prophets, tepid-Pope friends.
Give me Catherine Doherty, yielding her end.

"I Never Knew You"
(MATTHEW 7:21-23)

Our grand gestures are worth nothing beyond themselves.
They announce and close the show with a graceful arc.
And though we're spent by the time the act is shelved,
where was the line between the truth and a lark?
Love doesn't need our flare, our personal stage.
"Whom God loves, He hides," say the French, which points
to "Jesus" for the man who's learned to ignore his age.
(What he gives for others will cost him, bone and joint.)
Let me lose myself in each day's given company.
Let the Blessed Sacrament transform me when I speak.
Let me flower in silence, alone, on bended knee—
when I'm crossed. My neck, unsleeve. My will, make meek.
Christ is, and we, like St. Catherine, are not.
When our houses list, we break into a trot.

Houses Built on Rock
(MATTHEW 7:24–29)

We hear the wisdom of God, but how well does it take?
We'll pray for a season, but soon we're off to fairs,
largely imagined, until missing steps, half-awake,
we return to a milky haze of motherly care.
Sleepy is, and does, and doesn't act as he should,
despite his foundation. His building skills are what
is at question: how well can he shave, bend wet wood?
He botches windows, and his door, like his mouth,
   won't shut.
What will he do when his Lord returns? Offer snails,
cite floods, the history of his hitching thumb?
He might claim, "Master, I only knew how to fail
when You pulled me from the song on passing rum?"
Jesus will put him in a headlock, say "Friend,
I didn't see Ghandi when I fashioned your end!"

Winning My Leprosy
(MATTHEW 8:1-4)

Some cures seem to take longer: prayer, a fast,
which would almost get me down to my proper weight.
If I need to be cured so badly, why does the past
smother the need, lead me with factious bait?
To deliver that sanguine virtue, humility?
The only virtue found in its absence! No doubt.
(I think He'll need more time so I can see,
give myself to the Truth—lose each easy-out.)
He'll finish this, I know. It might take some years,
what with all that ritual cleansing He'll have to do,
giving me time to cow my childish fears—
to do my part—to cleave my sin from the view.
I'd gladly show the priests what's become of me,
if I could calm and win my leprosy.

A Man under Authority
(MATTHEW 8:5-13)

The King of time, amazed. How could that be so?
Did He have to walk blind because we need to see
Him humanly restore creation; or to know
How limited our sight is, how small, our burdened decrees?
And the Centurion? Perhaps he'd heard the gossip
from this servant, a member of this desert's tribe.
Maybe he'd seen zealots pray while being whipped.
Something in them made his world come alive,
though he loved his slave too — with a simple broken heart.
This Jewish God-walker, Miracle, offered more
than Roman statuary. The man wanted no part
of a fractured whole. (Each mine is judged by its ore.)
He bowed before the better man, would take
a place he knew. Nothing was his to make.

Mothers-in-Law
(MATTHEW 8:14–15)

The jokes come easy here; the only way
He could stop her from complaining was to heal
her latest cause. But she doesn't get that say.
This lamb, whom Peter must leave, prepares a meal.
Healing wounds so old they've become cliché,
He opens young (notable) scions. We bud in Him.
But whatever became of her, did she replay
the scenes long after, her life, by then a hymn?
Did she feel confirmed at unsurprising news,
God still, and always, followed by backward man?
Did she foreknow Zion's martyrs from the pew
of her kitchen window, each lover of Truth's last stand?
Our lives are like laundry, hang in an empty sky,
as Jesus prepares, through the years, our waiting eyes.

Judgment
(MATTHEW 8:16–17)

This was not the pompadour right, no sleight-of-hand
sideshow. How rowdy things must've gotten! The hairs
on the back of the whole region's neck had to stand
on end as all who prayed were paid at this fair.
(Think of future hawkers! The possibilities!)
New limbs on display, the unrestrained good cheer,
though the Lord, bearing our infirmities,
foreshadowing what was to come, had to hear
the talk: "a Davidic King," the zealots's read
of Him. "But can he manipulate this renown?"
Jesus was gone before He'd learned to lead—
to the next crowd, banquet, piquing small town.
The years would go fast, because Truth doesn't wait.
He comes in a flash, catches the world in a state.

Wherever You Go
(MATTHEW 8:18–22)

What did He see in the first? The blinds of ego?
A disciple, needing to sway the rudder's arc?
If so, Truth gave "Noah," a corrective blow:
he who wants to leave one, could fix on an inner mark.
And the next, was he lost in self-promoting wings?
Did he think the twinkle of gauds would help him see?
Jesus cut to the beating heart of things,
past platelet and bone, to that lie: self-pity.
He had no time, was busy creating each day,
bringing Narcissus to the pond, sweeping
each cottage clean. The Truth will only say
Itself, not schemes. Find it, and you'll hear weeping.
Though we are slow, He never sends us away.
He gives us the ears to live with the things we say.

What can You Say to the Sea?
(MATTHEW 8:23–27)

What do you say when God so shatters the known
that you're left with nothing, shards of who you were;
not during the storm, but in the quiet, each bone
wet man, left with a past that hasn't occurred?
This is how poverty starts, with just you and Him
and the flimsy material world, surrounded by souls
you know you're here for, by depths you can only skim—
the tricky night, without recognizable shoals.
This is why pennies matter, on the ground.
so you might pick them up, and be amazed
at a God who so manipulates each found
moment that any task can become, oddly, play.
We know nothing beyond the God who has us here.
And duty? It sounds like jazz to opening ears.

On a Theme Lifted from C. S. Lewis
(MATTHEW 8:28–34)

They asked Him to leave! Too many pork chops and choice
spirits perhaps: a large world, exposed
to view, with "appointed times," hellish voices.
Property had been destroyed, ex-thugs in repose.
They didn't want that. They wanted the coins they knew,
an almost peaceful place, with Rome on edge.
It was sorrowful, yes, but the corn and the children grew.
Let those pigs be the last to test that prophet's ledge.
And what could Jesus do when fools bid Him go?
He left them to their shrinking illusion of "town."
The time is always short, and a hungry wind blows
before and after that piggy, truth, is drowned.
Without our God, we scatter back to the sea.
Pigs and people trade places, become one species.

Jesus Blasphemes
(MATTHEW 9:1-8)

Jesus is the tense He alone makes: a present
so alive with healing, heaven's economy
that He fences the faith of friends for the cripple's, bent
in paralyzed fear. "Virtue" he says, "is free."
Teaching the moment to time, He utters Mercy,
giving His voice, two hands to His mortal good.
But the scribes have rules to right them; they disagree.
(Pilgrims need code to get through the darkened wood!)
So Jesus, like a teacher trained for the job, uses aids:
calls forth the man, so that even the deaf might hear.
The multitude rejoiced—watched their leaders fade.
They marveled, as the end of time, in Love, drew near.
But how can I love Him, this God who gives such joy,
with my shoeboxes, pockets—the spotted hands of a boy!

Matthew, in the Counting House
(MATTHEW 9:9)

Matthew was in his counting house, counting
on vacations—the days away from minding the sore.
The sky was blue, so he lunched outside, mounting
with birds who returned too soon to a dying shore.
But then His voice! Living, internal waters
startled alive the sea in its promise: life.
Matthew's plans vanished like the illusions they were.
(He quit his job—for abstractions, a heavenly fife!)
It made him laugh. There would be dues, but he'd pay
for his choice, because what could he lose but this
    mangy fleece
called life? The world could take it every day:
a coat that would wear you, down, its own police.
Unless we are called, how can we come up chosen?
We'd sit between movements, never put our toes in.

Matthew, with Sinners
(MATTHEW 9:10-13)

Matthew was amazed to see his part of town
so transformed, with rabbis, women of the night.
This Jesus wasted no time in bringing down
their noses, to smells as real as "spiritual blight."
"Yes, inhale, my friends, because who of us can tell
what sways each viper's nest, the human heart....
And how will I know this master's vision from hell
if my only guide is his sorcery, his art?...
But that voice! Again, it comes from a different place—
where mercy rules, where scribes are made to kneel....
But will this sweeping change leave a lasting taste?...
Well, prison always ends with a last good meal!"
Humility was the only, and sane way to go.
He knew that, but not how far he'd have to row.

New Wineskins
(MATTHEW 9:14-17)

God honors what He's made: the exertion of sweat,
sustained. Like call and response in church or jazz,
the human gets to work with God, who lets
the dialogue happen in fallen time. It's as
little Thérèse once told me, lifting her shift
to turn: "Yes, I have done this," her life, a bold
template to be matched, challenging me with the rift—
as if weak prayer, an alembic, might make wood gold.
My technique is weak—old fiber, shrunken cloth,
too frayed to hold a stitch. So I welcome her hand,
will try to be open to every passing moth.
(I'll work hard, try to build a lemonade stand!)
Thérèse, take my hand, I'll be your eighth-grade child:
I'll walk next to clicking beads, in single file.

Keener
(MATTHEW 9:18–27)

The flutists were wrong! And if they were wrong about
    death,
they were wrong about everything else. And so are we.
We don't know life, nor God, nor why we are left
feeling stranded here, without an anchor of sea.
How could we know less? Oh, we march around with
    our canes,
talking this, waving, buying and selling goods
which are the flotsam of life nearly lived, a strained
bluster, to keep our bearings, what's understood.
The old woman, the ruler, though, knew what those
    who feed
on suffering do: that insistent flesh is a rod.
And appearances? For dandies, fops. Real need
drove them to crawl on the ground to a passing God.
Complacent wisdom, at end, will get put out.
Let my soul rise raw, in the elements of doubt.

Mary's Eyes
(MATTHEW 9:28-31)

Since no one could see them, the blind men didn't care.
With walking sticks against a hemmed-in night,
their off hands, helping to shout His Name in the air:
they called and their future rose, gave them second sight.
Like new coins, their eyes! And all they'd felt, they now
could touch. Jesus tried to keep them in line,
because they didn't know Whom to praise. They bowed,
then tried to settle in, these heavenly signs.
But red sun now saucered the water! The cliffs were aflame!
Like kids on the last day at school, they hopped
and rammed into one another, each wanting to claim
the road. Jesus smiled. Who knew when they'd stop?
Deferring, Jesus wants the incense to rise.
And the Father? He'd given that Baby Mary's eyes.

"He Casts Out Demons..."
(MATTHEW 9:32-34)

When language itself gets the better of them (they try
to find some higher ground), they sound the fool.
They might've found solace in silence. But they'd never
 plied
that trade. They were busy running an imagined school.
There is no recorded response, though we can imagine
Jesus leaving them His absence, the quiet,
the wind, a few scraps of parchment lifting their sin
for a moment in the temple, no one left to buy it.
We all get those moments, don't we? When we see
 how short
we fall. (We lose that slightly bigger us.
They're much too late now to gather other retorts!)
Their lot now is to sit with themselves, their dust.
When I pump your hand, friend, be sure to talk some sense.
My need is, like Mercy, a toothy picket fence.

Bound by Two Hands
(MATTHEW 9:35–38)

He was God, but bound by two hands, He couldn't reach:
the crowd harassed by lies which feed on their lives,
every packaged demand for money's deserted beach,
the hope that won't come before the goods arrive.
Mass, likewise, can seem more promise than answer,
but as people get closer to their unleavened Host,
God takes His rightful seat. His quiet stirs
the flame, through each lifted voice — our only boast.
And because only children can open heavenly doors
as wide as God, a hush starts to settle each man
who, face-down, bows on marble, heaven's floor.
(And the long game rises, changes the lay of the land.)
Prayer makes what's coming a given: a rose, an itch.
We wait in His lush green porticoes, with the rich.

No One Else has ever Spoken Like This
(MATTHEW 10:1-16)

We're never quite ready, are we? He pays postage, sends
us in twos. (We're stamped by an attending angel!)
We go because we're sheep, no shield to defend
us, no money either, no chance for any gainful
recompense. No one's ever walked this ease;
as if the world were passing, has had its sway,
like He could adjust whole cities just to please
us, in The Spirit of God who makes every way!
"Go . . . Be wise as serpents, as gentle as doves.
Be poor, expect disgrace; but proceed, since you know
My Father. Everything passes away but Love."
Move like you've got the room to stretch and grow.
Sifted, we're graced in God's transparency,
which is wide enough for this world, till it chooses to see.

Saints are Never Sure
(MATTHEW 10: 17-25)

You'll meet kings. And then He drops the other shoe:
their swords. This is how badly people want Truth,
who's the Pope's poodle — until He crosses you.
Then they'll come at you with a devils' tooth.
All part of the irrevocable plan of God.
He gives us His word, another world, which might
appear to those on the fence an unseemly rod
since it spares the enemy, his encroaching night.
But we've been that bully, too; it's the baggage we bear
(as we write our lives in dust, on pilgrim feet).
We don't always detach ourselves from the hostile care
we give, to wounds or to cavils in the streets.
Both the privileged and those wearing points can find
   a home.
Saints are never sure. They can't read the tome.

Do not Fear
(MATTHEW 10:26–33)

It's the extent of their slight that helps the saints.
They learn who they are in an accusing darkness;
all their lives they work for Jesus who speaks, acquaints
them with sloth. (They fall short, despite His success.)
Original sin, the rotted porch, their beginnings
are there at the end.... But hasn't He always danced
most cleanly among what's broken, in the light, offering
the only way — a sparrow's song, repentance:
everything that's dun-colored, small? Our gut,
response, must indict us, in each denial,
in all of what we don't say, and in the most of what
we do. (Our efforts can't erase those traces of guile!)
John Vianney asked Jesus to show him his every sin;
Weeks later, he stopped up his ears against the din.

Bad (Older) Parents
(MATTHEW 10:34–36)

Younger, we didn't gall ourselves, tried to be stout:
fought bad family with a martyr's flames.
A slower verb, we tried to burn "virtue" out.
(That started right after they got their Baptismal names.)
As they started to grow, a priest would almost cuss
us for their cavernous last pew daily Mass
behavior. (They could wake the dead, crawling on us.)
Rust on our older Toyota, we sought for tacit
control. My Down's guy once splashed in his glorious pee
with both hands in the pew at Sunday Mass. A kid
behind us pointed—though his excessive glee
was a bit much. Kindly parents didn't look. That undid
the new-parishioner damage—though my daughter's
   not Confirmed.
At twenty-seven, autistic; still our hope is firm.

No Father
(MATTHEW 10:37–39)

No father can be enough. He's a masted ship,
serving in place, almost directing the craft.
He's a hope, not realized, mapping each trip,
with blankets and trail mix, maybe a gangster, George Raft.
Once a fishwrapper, he's as flawed as his sons. They
    come whole,
unlike his daughter who wouldn't settle for that, sails
to know. She wends her way between wrecks and shoals.
He knows he won't be here very long—each gale
will point them home. They'll trek through pew after pew,
each ego making its unreasonable demands.
(The trials of fallen natures are never news.
Their spouses will love til they can barely stand!)
A house is a nest of crucibles—where we must die
each day and gratefully count the reasons why.

The Clown's Red Nose
(MATTHEW 10:40–42)

Life's an echo chamber—this is an advantage
for the close-behind! We can shadow, badly mime a
    knowing
King: His velour, calm lace. Royalty engages
the poor in the mere rustle of worked clothing.
We sing His gold, His wine; His voice, like water,
runs a clear fall day, owns us. We're happy to bow,
can learn from all we're not. (I could take my daughter!)
Not alone, we are the children of His vow,
of what we still might become. What step could be less
important than ours? Who could ferris wheel our way;
only grace can give us so little to confess.
Only grace keeps us this busy, walking His days.
We are one of many when we venture to speak,
can only sound ourselves in the world we seek.

Feasting with Fallen Women
(MATTHEW 11:1-15)

Feasting with fallen women: upon what scrolls
was this written? And if distantly on theirs, why;
did the law have to die? Was he on these prison rolls
for helping the chosen to heave a collective sigh?
Jesus loves him, asks him to stand down, to know
less: people were being raised, posturing spurned.
Then God offers glittering summation: this crow—
he was the ragged way, a realized turn.
He names him the greatest of saints, the start: the Baptist—
an Elijah, the waters of heaven tell people to love
this violence. It's the kiss of the Christ, the list
of the Father, the quietly shaped wings of a dove.
When heaven comes, what has been passes away.
The scratching and cooing of God: that's here to stay.

"To What shall I Liken this Generation?"
(MATTHEW 11:16-19)

Each generation must see itself in the doubts
and gleaned wisdom of their clan: their wife and children.
Which makes sense since this is where insight gets
    worked out.
Perhaps God judges no one. He leaves that to wrens,
to what's left of the fall, who stay busy playing neys,
who use old brooms to dance dead leaves away.
It's the open sea they reject: where they wanted to play.
And the Baptist! His bald lament had no cachet!
(He was so alive that they had to murder Him!)
Jesus, take what we know, our self-conscious art.
Give us a heart for what's always new, a slimmer
us, a gentle spirit—to play our part,
because wisdom comes alive in childlike deeds—
between a rocking horse and the needle's feed.

So, You're Saying there's a Chance?
(MATTHEW 11:20-24)

Might a sprig yet bloom in Sodom, might those singed hills
crack in ash, offer it (and us) new ground?
We think of smoldering chars, and salt, a bill
that can't be paid — but this quote might turn that around.
Chorazin! Paris! The shafts of ruined concrete,
buildings, as they sheer down, plummet, their descent
taking out cars, hotdog carts, the street!
(Could the bad look up, from a seedy bar stool in Lent?)
Tire and Sidon, and the crumbling salt of Sodom
serve their purpose today. Which helps us all,
because who's done nearly enough? Thy kingdom's
   crumbs —
Thy will be enough. (Jesus makes personal calls!)
If you've lost, look for butts in gutters, food on the street.
He's the only One you'll meet there — with holes in
   His feet.

For Jude, at 10
(MATTHEW 11:25-30)

Driving next to my Down's son Jude, I say,
"You know, I'm really not very learned." He replies,
"Me neither, Dad." He is a prophet, his days
a fight to embrace humility's proper size.
It's a road upon which we all must learn to walk,
and who better to teach me — ear to smiling ear?
His impeded speech might be prelude to real talk,
since I need to clear away noise to try and hear.
He pits the Mountaineers against the Seahawks;
sock cousins dance, his index fingers have names.
He wants the lively thing, can giggle and squawk
when he jokes, without guile. I struggle to do the same.
The Father swims in the strokes of His eager Son.
He races with Him until time itself is undone.

As Supple as Grain
(MATTHEW 12:1-8)

When He picks the grain, His ruddy sinews cord
the wheat, made of the self-same stuff! How could
He be concerned with niceties, with their lord?
The world was only real from where He stood!
But since the contrary twist in their grasping—He waits:
spells out the King's history, chapter and purse:
David was hungry, and so, with God, he ate.
(Imagine: a stalk of sky, its yellow burst!)
Their "temple," though, was bones without a heart.
Hollowed by surfeit, by an idol's scriptural breath,
they couldn't deliver Mercy, couldn't jump-start
their lives, deliver the Sabbath's eventual death.
As supple as grain beneath the open hands
of Love, the temple widens—as does the land.

Alphonse Liguori's Meditations on Death
(MATTHEW 12:9-14)

"So, then is it lawful for one to cure today?"
On what planet could healing cause a snit?
On ours — where the Truth seldom gets a say.
The dying stay busy trying to strangle it!
So He presents a lamb. Most people would brave thorn
or brake to help one — then dismiss the pat on the back!
Or think of soft moss, where a baby could be born!
This heartens us as logic can't do. But we track
down (kindly) subversive ideation when
it comes to symbolic error. Give an agenda
bully an inch and he'll take your life — then
you can watch the scribal dance. (It's pure dada.)
It's like too many twisted limbs, the path
beneath. Liars won't leave it, or their wrath!

In His Name the Gentiles will Trust
(MATTHEW 12:15-21)

He didn't brawl, or make noise, or cry out "need."
(He withdrew, walked with nature — for the few.)
Organic, He would sway in His text, a reed,
creating its way, each step, limning the blue
skies which remake each summer's startling day.
He healed, waited as the days decided
how each would go. This is why He walks this way,
to hear what the universe has to say, to abide.
We learn to follow His peaceful, echoing path.
Mostly Gentiles — no "people" to define our pain.
We trust in Him, taking cataracts for baths.
(When we sleep, His voice sounds like soft rain.)
Who would you rather entrust your penances to?
He is mercy, while allowing you to be you.

Catherine's Clemency
(MATTHEW 12:22-32)

Dogged at every turn, the Pharisees
needed a win. But the Spirit, who moves through all things,
can never deny Itself. It won't ration seed,
nor power. No, nor the somatic joy It brings.
Our antagonists here, the kings of convolution,
however, choose the smaller world. So the Lord
presents, as gifts, their sons, a simple homespun
truth — their fatherly reach. In dim accord
they watch God eclipse them in their domestic church,
in the valued other — because no one has a chance
of doing good alone! Clemency perches
in Her children's lives, sets up a heavenly manse.
Wisdom can only roost, find its place with kin.
You have to give up the rouse, let the chickens in.

By Its Fruit
(MATTHEW 12:33–37)

You see it clearly in nature: good trees, heaven's fruit.
Seeds are like little hatted peasants; this town,
city. They attract fresh air. Jesus's new suit—
your size! Intimate outdoor tables abound.
Sunny words here find a swing. The park is good,
as is your parish, my neighbor Mark. (We endure
the world.) What needs to be is understood;
the ham, like our compound sins, is slowly cured.
Our talk will define us—if we can stand some strain!
(If we try to bring people together, our hopes will rise.)
This world or the next, you can get there in some rain.
This is what lives inside of us—a cry.
No cloven hoof ever picked a piece of good fruit.
What's His endures because our "ends" become moot.

In the Eyes of Men
(MATTHEW 12:38-42)

The Pharisees want a sign as large as they:
a sprung floor perhaps, to preen like ballerinas.
They need time to stretch, to do hip rolls. These days —
their stature could make them sing. They are the because
of things, after all.... Jesus offers a ghosting town:
lost people, a history play, scenes near enough
to shake them — Sheba, Solomon, and Jonah — whose
    crowns
now litter the ground. (They were made of sterner stuff!)
The southern Queen had only Solomon as guide,
and yet she changed when she met that shadow of Truth.
Her heart became like the sandy sea. She vied
and waited for God's healing rain, His painted booth.
Truth carries us. We have no realized say.
We move in Mercy, day through forming day.

This World We Live In
(MATTHEW 12:43–45)

An unclean spirit, cast out, can find no rest,
no distraction. His hands are left to ply his bones;
this drives him over dry places where each test
fails itself. He bludgeons dark song, cutting stones.
Grinding his teeth, he returns, to more order than
before, more places to shred the him he feels
inside, more bitter, ugly ways to ban
others. He rages, his spirit cannot congeal.
Seven reminders join him. He can hate more then,
in more varied ways; their shrieks can almost save
his life, as they tear his spirit, each face, spend
their bodies, stomping on each other's grave.
So shall it be, Jesus says, with this wicked pack.
They can't let go, think to spike what they can't retract.

Mary's Moon
(MATTHEW 12:46–50)

Speaking to heal, He faces enemies who rue
neither death nor truth. They'd rub His face in their earth:
"Your mother, Moses — she needs to speak with You,"
as if, sinless, they could define Him, birth
themselves. "And who is my mother?" He asks the
    lame....
"The obedient one.... Look at her face; see who
she is before you try to give her a name."
(Only those bearing the Truth can walk what's new.)
The Father's will gives creation its face. Completed,
that world brings the kiss of Jesus, and each bit
of our beings respond! Each attended moment led
His brothers to her! (This is how each candle gets lit!)
No speech should advance us, no pose should give us more
than we have. The stars, Mary's moon, the shore.

The Whole Came First
(MATTHEW 13:1-9)

Jesus went out of the house and sat by the sea!
Was it a cool morning? Did the lapping waves
sooth, smooth stones—the Father's eggs! A free
morning sun, mist. His robe moved a breeze. That saved
Him in its small way. Soon folks peopled the place,
had Him sit in a boat. (They seemed to Him like a field
of grain, or the crumbling soil beneath, traces
of what would come!) Most yakked, their lives like creels,
after the catch of the day. So He spoke about seeds—
said the soil came first. If they didn't work their hearts,
how could they expect growth: meet the world, their
    needs?
(The whole speaks itself, always gives rise to its parts.)
One wakes up in the morning, and what does He see?
The heart of the Father, the place He makes for the trees.

Madonna House, Walmart, and Stevens
(MATTHEW 13:10-17)

Why hide? Because people are too quick to see.
They come His way because they have these baskets
which need filled, to the brim with more of what is empty.
(We can feel that sometimes, in the frozen lot. We forget
where we parked our car. We have to traipse — never
easy!) Walmart becomes facade in winter —
it's like trying to carry eight plastic bags in sever
cold. Bitterness conspires against our blood; no fur
is enough. The compounded icy silence shivers:
we hear "the nothing that's not there." Prophets,
we welcome Stevens's noh-world. (Ontario river
ice loudly cracks. We listen, are ready to let
the Lord have His way. Let the world utter His name.)
You have no status; that's the reason why you came.

Where Colored Doors Can Close
(MATTHEW 13:18–23)

Don't receive by the wayside. Find a place away
from well-lit taverns—where your thirsty heart, or His,
can find a good banjo, or rutabaga. (Stray
from beneficial microbial life!) In business,
Avoid stoney, rootless places. Tubers are thin,
short here, hold little water. Be still, then choose
Mary's earth. If your plants survive both kith and kin—
their happy hands, takes—you'll know how to lose.
And lastly, beware of thorns, the obvious signs—
cities, bright light nights, the happy loot.
Find modest neighbors, on both sides, combined,
where you'll find smaller-sized indigenous fruit.
Good ground! You only find that here. God knows,
and is doing a Mary-telling, where doors can close.

"Parker's Back"
(MATTHEW 13:24–30)

Stories happen: a silly man sows good seed.
(He wouldn't be worth following otherwise.
Good intention always fails in these kinds of reads.)
We root for his sorry planting, wait for his rise.
Early, when he sleeps, his enemy hums her hymn.
Christians are always the worst here! They shop at bad
bistros; their caramel coffee overfills, past the brim.
She deserves no champion here. (She has no dad.)
Wisdom, of course, saves our man, as together
or apart they'll have to grow. That's the wheat—us.
And so, despite this Byzantine plot, in this feather
gentle tare-tale, his heart must build on trust.
We get the binding, the burn—a couple's story.
And why not? Jesus is a pervasive glory!

Mustard Plants
(MATTHEW 13:31–33)

God's ways can be unwieldy, unattractive too;
weedy limbs can cry "friend," pushing through air,
making small homes. Their yes is bird-shelter, true—
because they will not conform. They are seven stairs,
each of their own making. Birds nest, track below.
The whole patch is a sprawl, a metaphor for God
in this created world. He takes your knowledge in tow,
then overwhelms it—too many birds, cats, cod.
You can never know what he's doing. Think of this leaven
maven. Like God, she stays steps ahead of the game,
makes the treasure rise—intent—seeding heaven.
Who could cover this, make aesthetic claims?
Inherence, and not our look, is what matters here.
Too many bent sticks in the winter woods to clear.

The Holy Hand Grenade
(MATTHEW 13:34–35)

Monty Python's HOLY GRAIL comes next—
the contorted repetition; "and without a parable
He did not speak to them." Perhaps Matthew, vexed,
"skipping ahead," was searching for a bearable
groove, counting to three, the unhappy weight
of a biblicalized style. In any case, the pearls
are uncovered. He "utter(s) things," a freight
"kept secret from the foundation of the world."
We, the spiritually lame, the functionally blind,
smack into necessary walls. (We refuse to see
the blue sky rive, the brighter hues behind.)
Without help, how can any of us learn how to be?
The verse does that here. It locates the reader,
the grace behind the words—it Lebanons the cedars.

Down Time
(MATTHEW 13:36-43)

The adrenaline, gone, the tremors fade away.
There's no holy wind to help them wash the dishes.
A piece of furniture slides. The fire, the day,
both wane in the thinning smells of olives and fish.
Christ, in His calm, explains. The Son of Man
must allow hell a home, a barrier reef.
Nothing is alien to Him or His Father. He'll stand
then — as now — in the depths of fire, belief.
His chosen clatter early, work for breakfast:
fishermen who've had trouble getting most
of this, having just danced to sleep; their sins cast
overboard, again, like offal: the life of their Host!
Bless the people we've hurt, too many to repay.
We live in forgiveness, keep what we throw away.

St. Pio's Pearl
(MATTHEW 13:44-46)

We are made to seek ourselves, to work on, to hide
the house we build. His Italian face didn't favor—
like Hollywood: scrub brush cinema. His laugh confided
in Pietrelcina. Humility had to labor
to produce this abused man—for the most part
it was envy, malice. (We're all called to do what we can!)
He hid his pearl. We, who mostly know false starts,
try to do the same! The answer must cost us our standing
among men; each one of us, more false than true.
We lack his humor, his brothers. We lack his rock
solid filmed face which will not change for you.
(He sees us even from there: nosey, taking stock
though we can't see.) Pray for us, new friend.
We want to orbit here, in that kind of end.

Jesus's New Earring
(MATTHEW 13:47-52)

The kingdom of heaven is like a taut gossamer net,
angels rapture fish—golden sweat on their brows;
they glass sand, make the trees a still life. The sun sets
on blue boats as seraphs toss the lost to sows.
Then Jesus shifts gears: much bigger messengers shovel
Dantesque souls into the furnace as they wail
their strange concerns—every idol, tongue, and goal,
each short term—no friends or crowd to offer bail.
Then the Word surprises, tells us scribes will treasure
the old—and the new! Some so much the former that
    no one
takes time to check out His nice earring, the pleasures
of licit flesh! Everyone there will be stunned
to see the hot rods: what is, what has been, good.
We'll hear new engines roar under pearly hoods!

On the Rooftops with Handel
(MATTHEW 13:53–58)

They knew His face. "Isn't he Joseph's son?
Are not his sisters poor?" So, established, they took
offense. God Himself had "branched" this town. (Not
   for dumb
show). Jesus was too bland to warrant a look.
His interests ran to sink holes, to the poor, housing—
whereas the chosen are marked, carry something of heaven.
The poorest don't muse on ends. They live in a grouse
of alleys, stained sinks (today). They are old leaven,
without the dough.... Those lies still fail us here—
because we die! Our persistent sins only seem
for sale. They mark us with Moses. (We marry fear,
our distress.) No gauze or salve can remake us, or stream
heaven. Jesus is like a reed, a tall candle.
He's in puddle mirrors, on English rooftops with Handel.

His Lizard Hands
(MATTHEW 14:1-2)

Herod thinks John must be risen from the dead.
(This happens because power, in the end, turns inward.)
Like a python muscling its long, thick body, spreading
its slithering girth, clearing a bookshelf, bored;
our king's an ouroboros — having eaten his spume
for so long he lolls, endures the soak of his fame.
He owns the castle's corners, each afternoon,
looks for completion. Herod plays mindless games,
hurts cats, can keep nothing down. He eyes young boys,
numbers the things he can do. The silk he wears
condemns him at every turn. (Everything's a ploy!)
He needs to ruin what he cannot bear,
rules a miniature kingdom, whatever its size —
until his lizard hands become a kind of prize.

Hell in Ringlets
(MATTHEW 14:3-12)

Herod celebrates his birth, for others,
of course, for Herodias — the girl; he plucks strings,
to find sensual memory, then thinks of his mother —
offering him sackcloth, ashes. (He could still be a king!)
Now it's a smaller woman who rules his desmesne:
a platter! He's wrapped her climbing hands in pleasure.
(He is, again, the nothing boy — what remains!
It all comes down to killing, measure by measure.)
But he'll miss the Baptist. (He'll never speak again!)
Herod grieves, he'll never know the roads he might
have traveled. He's now a captive to fleeting friends: —
a nocturne, tragic, a stranger in each night.
He howls to hell before his time ever comes:
a drooling idiot who must watch his thread being spun.

What John had Planted
(MATTHEW 14:13-21)

Grieving for John, alone, Jesus laps out
in a boat. Soon people follow Him on foot,
donkeys. It's the maw of this lunacy, this doubt
that contend. Quietly, He touches His side, in the soot
of evening. Making the first star brighter, He offers
the Baptist: "Give them something to eat"; God's reign
would not be dimmed by Herod, purloined by furs,
the forests of venality, those dead to the pains
of the living. (Jesus would bask children in light!)
Twelve holy baskets, for each apostle who'd follow
Him. Baskets after baskets would give people their sight;
each answering death's grab, its pitched and hollow
lie. He would offer His Father's risen heart.
If they didn't know the end, they could learn how to start.

"To Make an End..."
(MATTHEW 14:22-33)

Life never gives what we need. Without Jesus,
the waves bark, the wind splinters the sail. He'd sent
the crowded disciples boating ahead. ("Keep us,
Lord.") He did this for the Baptist—bent
the storm, would've done more, but those dear faces,
their unrealized fears. So He surprised them again
with an in-your-face miracle. Torn from his traces,
Peter jumps from a boat—a would-be leader of men.
He fails. That is our way. That's why they call this
a journey. And what did he think, wet, blanketed?
It was always the first day at school here—in the hiss
of self-reproach. (How much Jesus could he get!)
All wet, we start anew, get closer to that.
Our end will adjust the beginning. He won't stand pat.

When the King Appears
(MATTHEW 14:34-36)

Friends welcomed Him with tilapia, raisin
bread, lamb, got this news: "He's walking the top of
    the sea!"
First asking permission, they made every house an inn —
just to see people pile in, each one set free,
as olive trees and wind completed each other —
invited every creature to touch His dusty robe,
all made whole, or close. (This new breeze should smother
them all!) Rabbis danced in the street. He'd broken
    the code.
It was like He both ended and saddled all of time.
What would the Baptist have made of this, this peace?
Would he have sat under trees, eating dates, feeling fine,
every ruffled hair smoothed, now part of a new feast?
In this world or the next, the normal ceases to matter.
When the King appears, what is held together tatters.

Hippy Law
(MATTHEW 15:1-6)

The house is for fewer people, much less room:
you gratefully graze against your spouse as you pass.
You appreciate her shoulder, feel night, law's loom.
The weave of this world binds you, in the grass,
around the next bend. These places save us—from speech.
The law there is as quiet as a hook
in a barn-fence loop, at twilight, both worn, having
    reached
the close of their day. We're thankful for the cook!
(There one can sometimes love freely, like the first hippy,
baptized at Pirates' Cove—truck a Malibu beach.
You'd be younger, of course, taking that first dip
in the holy ocean, some answers, still out of reach.)
Mercy's the first mother, Mary in madras.
She loves against the grain, without the fuss.

Waiting Loudly (in Glasgow)
(MATTHEW 15:7–11)

We would re-plant, tamp ourselves into better versions:
a Vatican diplomat, perhaps, or an aide de camp.
We'd come from happier homes, quieter dispersions.
We might even, now and then, speak the beautiful, amp
the good.... Not likely, we're the cold truth we each
must deliver: sometimes Pharisaical, made for
today, a forked tongue searching for Spirit's speech.
(Who we might be, behind two game show doors!)
The heart is where we must start from—in ignorance,
    trust.
We might yet know silence, be people who want to become
like Jesus. (You try not to hear yourself on the bus,
Whitman lost in traffic, Ginsberg's dynamo hum.)
Park benches provide us with rough seats in the rain.
A stranger will come. You'll chat near Scottish cranes.

The Truth must Shock Us Blind
(MATTHEW 15:12–20)

The scribes never planned on falling in ditches—the chide
that lies are when you speak them in the night.
Their end cries them. Their followers won't. Each ride
ends the same. Shallow echoes, the stinging bite
of empty seats.... When we choose a shorter us,
we, too, must take our scourging, our purgative walks—
in sackcloth, quiet as moon dust, prairie husks.
We learn to be thankful, our lives, outlined in chalk.
Then gratitude can sing like birds, the whole morning.
We can't be worthy of what we can't own. Our hearts
would paint us a desert—but one is already forming.
(On good days we wake and find our earthly art.)
The Truth must shock us blind or it's not real.
A wild animal, It forages twilit fields.

Parents
(MATTHEW 15:21–28)

Jesus departed, nothing but a lost cur
following Him in the cool Tyre morning, true
in its way. One could always count on flesh, fur,
Eliot's feces. (The dog circled what it knew.)
"Send her away!" the apostles cried, since the woman
didn't count. (Like one of those city dogs—who'd taken
no part in the fall, she hoped the next sniff might mend
her world, community, offer a side of bacon.)
Totemic, she waited on His word, His drum.
Word salads didn't matter, only what signs
her Master would give. So she sat, like a dog—in sum:
she would worship His will. She would sit up, align
for crumbs to bring her lost daughter home.
To her, focus was fact—the teeth of a comb.

What We're Made For
(MATTHEW 15:29–31)

Jesus clambers a small mountain, sits down to transfigure
the moment—at His ease. A surprising pose for a King,
but life is new here, His tenderness—a rigor
which comes from a fasted heart. He hums, starts to sing.
The needy eventually come, from back countries,
from the bean fields, because lies can't last forever:
disordered voices—all the hatreds they couldn't see.
God has called them. They could feel that, and so severed
themselves from money, the busyness of the devil.
The quiet burned that away, His fingers to faces.
He healed because He was health, high on a hill,
creating children. Themselves again, they paced,
hopped, laughed; they could have been a morning, or bees.
They knelt because they have these kinds of knees.

The Rest of the News
(MATTHEW 15:32–39)

The disciples gathered the fragments, the wilderness,
put both together. On a mountain (their past), want
led to others, a bigger slice of life: the rest
of the news was the person right next to you, a font
of recovery; more than, they counted, four grand—
men, their kids, a woman's fresh air. People sat,
cared for by the insistent, opened hands
of Love. And when it ended, many rolled their mats,
walked down the mountain, sang for all they were worth.
Nearby trees seemed more vibrant. Each housed a miracle,
a tone; some named one, circled it, then birthed
a forest. A silly one, when life is full.
Next, the small group gathered, a rocking boat:
Magdala. The world sang, the song had notes.

When Signs Ask for One
(MATTHEW 16:1-4)

They were willing to play, to treat Him as an equal.
After all, they too were people of influence, mattered
(generous fields of swaying wheat, God's sequel).
Humble, they saw themselves as water, a patter—
vibration in the holiest of glasses!
So God became the room: He was the world
that would wake them up—sky's blue, the water's, grasses,
without the burden of fame. Truth always curls
like falling leaves. Lesson number one: they are
not Him, nor can they keep up. They need to hear
the sounds of the world that bends them! Jonah's star
still reaches, spans epochs. Did they hope to steer
this whale? We need to see what we do to people.
We take the good, skewer it with a steeple.

The Multiplication
(MATTHEW 16:5–12)

It was fitting, the apostles getting stuck on bread.
Maybe that's why they'd hurried, forgotten to bring it.
(He loved their panic threshold, their sense of dread.
They'll feed everyone in sight, keep the candle lit!)
They pleased Him, compared to the glib Pharisees.
No leaven could raise that bread. (His own would plump
out nicely!) The oven of love gets room to free
the gas, open the sugar. They'll work, they'll hump,
route accepted sense. Nothing made to taste!
Their response would arch a doorway; time would know.
It would involve a Passover Host, every caste
and battered nation. They'd have miles, eons yet to go
before their sleep. Our takes and desires have to calm.
Like them, we must sit until done, cool under palms.

The Son of the Living God
(MATTHEW 16:13–20)

The book continues: "Who do you say I am?"
Peter, never one for half-truths, gets it right.
(The title was not a new invention, crammed
into the text, as no one questions the phrase.)
And Peter is immediately rewarded—
would act in His stead! (Jesus would have to leave him—
his tears, his hands. Then he would have to ford
dark rivers, learn to play flute and not his brain stem.)
Each apostle had a future that was drawing near;
they had to see who they were, how they would fit,
since Jesus's language here announces, veers
into the future—where fires had to be lit.
But why the silence, why the hidden plan?
Like everything else, the whole show makes the Man.

Our Notion, Our Fuss
(MATTHEW 16:21-23)

Jesus needs to draw out our best. (There's no winning here.)
Each man must learn to live through death, the turns
only Mary's disciple-heart was able to bear.
And fear begins to crowd them — as they hear Him burn
His answered "yes." That's how, in the end, He'll know us,
like Peter, in his first Papal decision. He says no.
We'll try to follow behind because we trust
the things that give us us. (Our lives say so.)
"Get behind me, Satan!" Jesus brutally (true)
says — and we'll see the comfortable lie we've been.
We'll stand, again, adjust, try not to rue
our course. We'll pick up after Peter, scour our fens.
We do not know the nails that wait for us;
we've known pain, drops on a skillet: a notion, a fuss.

The Help We Get
(MATTHEW 16:24-28)

Peter's heart, like ours, was not enough, and that's
why we need it to be. (Can a small cove be enough?
Or a small fire we build?) Those needs dig at,
enlist others. But there can only be One, a rough
estimate of how we need to proceed. He lives
everywhere, in fogged barns, in Thérèse's flowers,
though each one perishes. (Our ancestors gave
it all back.) That saint gave up her personal tower,
needed gangrene to make her whole. She shares:
"That was a good; no one else should share His glory" —
though angels do! (Who knows what we'll have to bear,
say yes to. Dark pages make for worthwhile stories.)
Did my grandma's (Celine) print on her wall send aid
when I asked for help as a child? Can those hearts fade?

The Book of Him
(MATTHEW 17:1-8)

Everything in this book is about who He is.
He's always creating Sabbaths, showing up, out.
We've all seen Him in one way or another; it's His
only way. (How else can we see what life's about?)
Say yes, and you get a mountain top, some day,
some way. Maybe you're walking to church, or your dog
sports alongside. Maybe you've had a fay
number of beers, and the fall vegetation clogs
a lamp-lit sewer—with a watery discourse. (Good brews,
companions that night.) Of course I already knew Him,
but that's just the point. It's all His reach, each crew
you've known. He's irresponsible! (You can't trust
Him at all!) You don't have to wait for Him to catch up.
He's already there, working on a rabbit hutch.

Elijah
(MATTHEW 17:9–13)

John didn't know his other name. Few do.
Heaven hands out new ones; all justice there —
no Pharisees, just an empty seashore, a few
happy gulls to allow each a sense of home. The bare
cross in the sand. It will provide gravity,
what they need to continue this walk. Then everyone
they meet will be Him — alive — in their eyes. The only
cities will open, the Father's palm, double sun
that ripples and rattles each unrepeatable day.
What did the two of them say under trees, with all
that shared insight? A third footprint — the dime
His Father spins! (The forming market stalls!)
Two wills can never converge. The tension speaks
who prophets are: sweet revelatory leaks.

Happy Dis
(MATTHEW 17:14–21)

Prayer and fasting, a two-step, deep in the echoing
nave of a purposeful being: a city with towers.
(A better Dis.) There are statues, coaxing Mary, singing.
It's a place where we know completion—vernal showers.
Here we right no wrongs. We don't leave His happy house.
You may be an older man, from a hayseed country.
You'll own nothing, no long-standing grouses.
Like here, He is what He gives, and He gives freely.
When the miracles finally come, you'll be late to know.
(It'll be God operating as He always does:
above, apart, familiar as morning crows.)
He alone, alive to made ways of wind-blown love.
This is what can happen when your Father's the King.
Love reaches—is happy to toast your road again.

The Lies at the Local Library
(MATTHEW 17:22-23)

The great King must die. It's in all the classic tales;
dark forests grow, whatever coheres must fall
to thorns. How else do we grow? Every success fails.
Or it would come down to us here: half-masters of stall
tactics. We must cry out in a pain that offers
no consolation! Every child knows this tale.
(Adults try not to ride that horse, or its spurs.)
But death is our final companion, owns us; our stale
denials induce sleep, a feast of lies.
If the King chooses to return, to sit on His throne,
He opens up the land for the young who try
the new, helps us to ignore jaded jugglers, the crone.
Children are fierce customers. They need to see.
They'll test things, each lie at the local library.

Peter Fishes
(MATTHEW 17:24–27)

First one fish, and then the other, (both startled)
each feeding, too far from the city of God! Perhaps
Jesus is a little amused at Peter's heart.
(It was always helpful to create a teaching flap!)
People miss God sitting before them. (They've livings
to make!) He'd wanted Peter to see this: how calm
settles each sea. He should live nowhere else. Giving
was the key. So there the Pope sat, tossed by balmy
trees. Did he need to bait his hook, he wondered?
Maybe he could just whistle into the deep.
He hated his talk, these questions, his private thunders.
How should he walk? What would he pull from his grief?
"What's due, comes! The miracle — we don't see that."
But why choose fish? Did He want to have a chat?

He Talked to Me
(MATTHEW 18:1-4)

A child lights up a bit in the elders' midst.
(He could matter here.) He watches every face;
his life, as always, is at their mercy, a fist
once — or a hand moving him into place.
But then he sees that more is happening here,
something he can't quite grasp. The leader is calm,
the only untroubled face. The others are steered
into that ease. But then the Man calls him a psalm.
The lad likes His eyes, His regard, gentle hand to His
    chest —
His peaceful face, His laughter. He also knows
what the men have to learn. The boy would follow the rest
of his life. (What good did he have? Just dumb shows.)
"Let my life take whatever's to become of me.
I'll follow — because He talked inside to me."

An End We'll All Face
(MATTHEW 18:5-10)

Our sins indict us, even after they're gone;
our names become real with each. (A hell is spun.)
It's too late to chop off a leg, to reach that dawn.
It's too late to cry out: "My sin makes me. I'm undone!"
What forgiveness could we possibly know in dark places,
where Confessional penances only remind us—of us.
We try to bear our burden, but hidden faces
coax our doom. We can never come clean. How can disgust
fade? Only Jesus Himself, after death, can burn
off that brand. It's us, in our unmovable places.
Francis, Pio, Kate feared hell, hadn't learned
enough. We are saddled with our sorry paces.
Jesus, only You can make this liar whole.
More than a beggar, I want to become his bowl.

The Delayed should be Allowed
(MATTHEW 18:11-14)

The delayed should be allowed to take to the fields —
as Jude does whenever he's at a fair. He could be
an archer, or climbing an inflatable, with shield
to king a mountain, because he wants to be free
in his life — to be someone with cowboy days.
But he is also just more alive than the rest
of us. His delight, hardly normal, gives him away.
He likes to try his hand. If he's not the best,
you see no scorn. (He's in.) And he smiled wide
yesterday when I told him he fans Jesus's
delight when he walks into a room. He rides
the Spirit. A man without any guile, he frees us.
He doesn't like his Down's, but wants our world.
But I wonder, could he change a room with that pearl?

Three Stories
(MATTHEW 18:15-18)
"MIRANDA OVER THE VALLEY"

What could I do but quietly insist on truth,
despite pressured superiors, sometimes in over their
 heads?
They saw her as an abandoned slut—their tooth
and claw. At the Dean's table, more odd than the dead
parents, dying boy in the story: I was
the only person there with a terminal degree
in lit. I knew I'd often failed—one does—
teaching. But it's the extent of the fear we see:
it's an anti-abortion story! In a Catholic school!

Most days went well. Even the student who lied,
(perhaps caught up in the mania, a fool's
orthodoxy) a theologian's daughter, denied
perhaps, her gold stars for that. Andre Dubus, forgive
us our holy nonsense, our brain-addled sieves.

Chićka Chićka Boom Boom
(MATTHEW 18:19-22)

When two hearts are one, a Third is always involved.
A wind might come up, rip across the surface of Mars.
(These are the things that make unity so.) We solve
our lives slowly—where no one is surprised by a scar.
We forgive because we have no choice. (We delve,
find the damage we've managed to do.) We confess, freely,
in Polynesia with what we can find of ourselves—
no applause needed, our guns under star-lit sea.
Seek forgiveness and the world's like a coconut tree!
It becomes peace-able, as you wait in your sigh;
which just means that things can never end here. We ski
friend, have a little hut, as angels fry
our eggs over-easy. We begin to learn each face,
carry some logs, some gourds—moon-lit grace.

Bosnia-Herzegovina
(MATTHEW 18:23–35)

The guide spoke: years ago, in a tobacco field
in Bosnia-Herzegovina, where a mom
could lay her babe in dewy furrows, steal
work-hours to buy some food. Those days were psalms:
parents everywhere finding ways to pay debts;
my dad, shook from the war, in an iron lung—
both sets, impersonalizing their regrets,
papoosing kids, taking things rung by rung.
Seven siblings, I was shielded from later violence.
We all have much to pay back—to our Lord as we crowd
around Him now, for our babes, our parents: that sense
of Mercy. (It vibrates when people live out loud.)
We gather to forgive, here in Medjugorje,
walking streets with rosaries, beading our glorias!

At the Carnival
(MATTHEW 19:1-12)

Marriage, we might say, is like a dance so young
only age can save it. No one gives lessons, and so,
if you're willing to take the lesser part, (sung
in what approaches two-part harmony), throw
in your ring. You'll have your chance to loop the cross:
share jokes, your art, become little as you go.
(Phariseeism gets sizzled here, boys get lost!)
You'll finish her ancient pop songs as you row
in the deep—nothing is hidden in this rapport.
I always need another chance to rebuild,
to listen closely, because I'm still paying her court,
(often) with cheer. (My begging cup—never filled.)
Sometimes in line my sins can seem to lessen.
This illusion fades, though, the closer I get to Confession.

Play
(MATTHEW 19:13–15)

The disciples cannot guide happy kids (as parents
know we sometimes must). Like little centurions,
they are play itself, spending energy, never spent,
as life creates bears and bugs, night trees. They're one,
inventing green, they surround us—camouflaged!
Jesus knows the song. Each (required) invented gift
is penumbra-ed in a tree-green unasked for squad:
the whirring wings, a summer breeze, all a mischief
never quite managed—so we can see. These clearly
define us. We get their energy and breathe.
Every bush face child revels here in yearly
(front-legged) song—they give us heaven. We're pleased!
Only Jesus is wild enough to swarm these kids.
(They both have green veins, can tell us what katydid!)

The Rose at Hand
(MATTHEW 19:16-22)

He liked the alignment idea, himself and Jesus;
he looked forward to playing the necessary bit part.
He would humble, avail himself. (He sees us.
So a pointed question might be the best way to start!)
Ready to bequeath, Jesus improved the man's sight,
gave him the second good he thought he had—
the real Lesson would wait. The man, lightened,
was ready to argue. So Jesus took the cad
and made things clear: life without real poverty
was always just approximation. Divest,
then start. Take the splintered cross, miles from where "me"
begins. (There's no victory without these tests.)
We're the clothes we wear, the colors that suit our needs.
They can swirl. For what's a pipe without a reed?

Old House
(MATTHEW 19:23–26)

Big money, overweight, can't win a footrace.
So it buys cordwood beech, turns those stacks into soldiers,
marches them through the wintery night. A grained face
turns back, weeps in the dark! The ghost of Dürer
is a busy German squall — a spent passion;
he moans before we reach Bayern, distances
mostly shadowed under the moon. You might shun
that holy place, invest in a purse. And the dance
of dark winds, the cries of the poor? That's Jesus's concern!
A man of influence, you might change the world,
but into what? Underneath, your wealth burns
its house. So you give a bluish lute, a whorl —
each lie running too deep. We build our keeps.
Pluck more strings, to compensate for the steeps.

These Popes
(MATTHEW 19:27–30)

He follows, loudly enough to count. Like Peter,
we pontificate, maybe shaving wood into curls.
(His wife's modest homespun tells him he either
works in the weather or sits with — his dear — the girls.)
Even today, he must reach his own, feed the poor!
Face it, these Popes are better than we — need to be.
Their sea is always pushing them far from shore.
Each's rigor will find the grace it needs to free
whole oceans. May that be our fate, as we gather behind.
Our concerns, of course, are smaller — the infestation
of earworms, the frass they leave in young green rinds.
Peters, older train engines, needs space, more station.
If we were to sail his ship, we'd undoubtedly fail.
The King takes us in, walking plank and sail!

Leaving Room
(MATTHEW 20:1-16)

Peter would have fallen on the sword, loudly;
he would've stormed or walked the battlements. He spoke
what he heard, died that way. He was born proud,
it was in his DNA. Even when he broke
at the end, he proclaimed Jesus — understood
by then, learned how to walk like the holy places.
Jesus loved that in all of them — how they would
turn, listen. Like John, who chose to hide his face.
He spoke less, was happy to walk where he could at
the end of the day. What kind of templates were these?
Like Mary, both were insignificant, meekly sat
at the assigned table. (They knew time from their knees.)
How else could He leave room for the rest, for you?
You, who've never belonged, whose readers are few?

The Time for Great Deeds
(MATTHEW 20:17-19)

Jesus gathered them, stopped, under a tree,
away from the carts, the noise. His friends needed
to hear this. He'd waited, for too long it seemed,
    spoke baldly,
pain on His face. The time for great deeds
was ending. (He spoke of himself in third person.)
"He will rise again." They each searched His expression.
He didn't tip them, tell them how to respond—that
    they'd run
like dogs, that they'd always be tested, learn how to shun
hatred. It would be a new world, where the chosen
were not, where most of the action in the play
would happen off stage. Where no one could tell who
    was in.
They'd begin the end times—gather the clay.
The riot starts along the side of the road.
A stone skips a stream; our ways begin to slow.

Thy Brothers' Elbows
(MATTHEW 20:20-23)

Two apostles wanted to sit at the front of the class,
legs extended, gangly elbows, big smiles.
Their Jewish mother wanted first ribbon—and fast.
(How bad things might have turned had they used guile!)
So Jesus, their teacher, offers the strain their grand
marquee would demand of them! Could they swim a
    dead sea,
could they mouth a tongue no one else could understand?
Could they bear the whip, the weight of all crosses, breathe
when their body said no? Their ambitious mother did
them in—and not. After all, they would know His sail.
Their chips were all in: a hope larger than sin.
(Tight behind Him, how could the brothers fail!)
Each step would matter as time began to close.
They had no worth outside of the path He chose.

For Yeats
(MATTHEW 20:24–28)

Rulers, lording, a beautiful loneliness waits
for you, must come. Like the poet, we belong
down there, on our marrow-bones, scrubbing. Yeats's
melody gets rid of everything else. It's a song
that chooses you! We make nothing happen. He comes
like a feather wafting onto a lake, like those swans
or Gregory's Coole Park trees: his bone-deep hum
rumbling (again) in your classroom. You, a don
in some other world. Such are the oral delights
of poverty. Nothing tangible, just a book,
tattered, the children you took those summer nights
to the public pool. That singing gives you a look!
When one commits to loss, he treks alone.
No crowd nearby—only Irish water, stones.

Keaton and Chaplin
(MATTHEW 20:29-34)

They could've been cow bells under the pale blue dye
of Palestine's sky; bone-dry hills—bereft.
Blind men give the world a tongue. Their cry
was a people, the ancient walls (what would be left).
They worked their twice blinded, sorrowful swaying
way toward Him, wondered: "What am I if You fail
me now; You've healed the others.... I'll have to pay
my way in at the blind men's ball.... I'll walk, will hail
my future, will die like a dog, in a lizard moan....
Ah, He owes me nothing! (What would that sound like?)
    My cries,
what I am; I'll shout until they pelt me with stones....
You made me, God. I repent for my greed, my sighs."
And so Jesus asked him, then healed both law and man.
The blind men wouldn't, at first, let go of his hands.

Donkeys Belong
(MATTHEW 21:1-11)

He's always doing this ridiculous stuff.
("Go to Pittsburgh and find a black moped on Fifth Street.
There will be bright yellow flowers, crimson puffs
of fairy dust on the tank, the key discreetly
placed behind the rear tire." No one has ever
done this—not to mention healings, in soft rain,
in Ireland, somewhere in Kerry.) But Pharisees never
change, do they: "Can I reconcile this with my gains?"
And so they miss the hope parade, the invasion,
the small chocolates that get passed out. (Someone
from the future microphones the holy occasion!
It's all been recorded!) Healings are supposed to be fun!
Did he laugh on his donkey under the palm-waving street?
Did His feet touch the ground? What kids did He pause
   to greet?

Children Take the Temple Floor
(MATTHEW 21:12-17)

When kids rule the temple's marble floor, the glum
high priests feel lost, defeated by the joy
of angels. (This is what happens when the columns
convert — as do the future attentive, the goy.)
"Out of the mouths of babes" praise knows no bounds.
It's God's ubiquitous laughter — a cheesy mac supper.
The King had finally come! He was Thompson's hound
from heaven, bounding back and forth, butt-
up, loving the mad giggles, the baby walks,
how their feet slap on the floor — perfection realized.
This is what we are made for; it's why the stones adore,
cry out. This is why we ride this pony prize
He brings. So let the scholars work out the rest.
Here the sky and the windy birds are the only test!

Dressed in Blue
(MATTHEW 21:18–22)

Jesus loved this time of day, morning almost
here. The houses, asleep. Wealthy servants outside,
in pens, collecting eggs. Some bread, toasted,
was in the wind. What would the Father provide?
Maybe some dipped in olive oil! The fig tree
didn't help. This might be one of those contrary days!
He touched the twisted trunk and foresaw the sea
of priestly ingratitude that would greet the rays
of the sun on temple stone: while the world, His flower,
opened. So He created food, then turned
to His hungry men. He was, after all, the power
that accelerates. (His apostles had much to learn!)
His morning sky and His mom—soon dressed in blue.
All that was left was to do what He came to do.

DRY SALVAGES
(MATTHEW 21:23-27)

One puts on a bowler hat for the part. The rustle
of success draws others in. Speech follows, if needed;
an audience always gathers. People hustle
over to see the great man. (Grace can't be impeded!)
So Jesus mans a Massachusetts deck.
He cares for fools, those both grim and risible —
loves the poor, the lost, the strewn, each solitary wreck.
(All people are what they need, made visible!)
Every poet must find a better way;
each must give away his plans, his sense of what is!
Jesus has something better, a new wife, a lay —
a future beyond the lapses of po biz.
Let the world try to drown us with its noise.
Silence lasts. It given us Eliot's buoys.

Harlots Who Go on Speaking
(MATTHEW 21:28–32)

The Baptist, his tax collectors, harlots, go
on speaking. (They will do so until they've been heard.)
It's the real world that stands up, late, against show.
They endure incrimination, the slow beard
of regret—which allows them room because they know,
have learned who they are. Their needed sins refine
them; while Pharisees loom, stack weights, bestow
the places of honor—as the unworthy, disinclined
sparkle, like cooled gold. These are, after all,
the children of John, the precursor. And isn't it so
that things hard won are more likely to stay—in His thrall,
to pass, limping, away from self, its woes.
Walk me, Jesus, with the others, behind,
where there can never be two of a kind.

O'Connor, Shouting
(MATTHEW 21:33–46)

Why did they never see themselves in these tales?
Maybe because He came from Nazareth,
or maybe because they could, and so had to rail
against a Him they could never be, the depths
they couldn't plumb. (Most of what we learn must
be unlearned, slowly, with surer hands! With fasting,
from — and for — our selfish hearts. Each bust
must be shattered, repeatedly, to form a lasting
trope. We must live, in short, like an opened sore.)
That's the only reason they kill: to keep what is wooden
hollow (and few): matryoshka dolls. A lore
that pleases them — as they try to keep what is good in.
If I'm all the noise I make, I won't hear much.
Like the blind we have to proceed in inches — by touch.

Pay Whatever is Due
(MATTHEW 22:1-14)

Who is the badly dressed fellow here? Let me see.
He comes in late, he's probably too loud!
He might start feeling his wine, having paid no fee.
(So I carry on, unaware that I dress in a shroud.)
This is the poetic lesson, the cautionary note
that won't go away. "Be silent," it says. "Grateful" —
so you can enjoy some life, in your quiet boat.
Forget what you think you know. You came late, full
of self-regard, remember? So sit quietly. Food
is a mercy, as is the bride. Let her beauty take,
relieve you of your sin. (Let your peevish, rude
ways pass you by. Enjoy the lake, the moon's wake.)
None of this has ever been about you.
Take what is given, then pay whatever is due.

Talkers
(MATTHEW 22:15–22)

They knew that one could always catch a talker
with talk. So they let out a line, pleasantly,
trying to put Him off His stride. (A balk
might give them an edge with the crowd.) But Jesus, free-
dom Itself, soars with an ease He always possesses,
answers them as if they were children. The coin
brought ease into the equation, a place where less is
God. Heaven can only exist if you choose to join
a quieter band, one which does not bandy itself
about like an answer. We are never that.
We are new-comers, after the second twelfth
apostle, after the saints, the dogs, a few cats.
Our ignorance will fill out the morphing list.
We're like trees in the unformed morning, a dewy mist.

The Sadducees
(MATTHEW 22:23-33)

The Sadducees idolized the steps of the law:
a miser's world, pecunious, a world of small hearts—
of tweezers and rice. They mistook a fence for the saws
which activate the quiet in man—the start
of life and living: Love's house. The Divine. He'd make
them who they were meant to be. But they wanted order,
one they could understand. They missed the takes
of Abraham, Isaac, and Jacob—who had no borders.
God revealed Himself in the open past, as he does
here, in marriage and out, in new clear days,
in places He speaks alive, in laws abuzz
in the humus that formed them. (It's what Love does
   with clay.)
Laws are like tender seeds. They crack, then open
in purity, like the waters widen in fins.

A Corpse's Flowered Jaw
(MATTHEW 22:34–40)

Awe was a gold earring the Pharisees could
not afford. They hadn't time for the ignorance
of small town prophets. They had to establish the good:
their place, their take — a movement without a dance.
Jesus, however, was time itself. He brought life.
God'd left His written way, yes, but that meant
He'd left poverty to scholars. (Believing in fifes
does not teach one to play!) It's the extent
of His love in us that matters. The words, the two
great hinges open and close the doors. They are
His anointing: a corpse's flowered jaw, the screws
applied every sunny morning. Books can look far
into the future, but they can only present.
It's self-abasement that erects the holy tent.

Nothing Comes Next
(MATTHEW 22:41-46)

They know so little, are ready for even less;
and their public humiliation can't help them. So
where do they go, to a Christ who is so blessed
that He's both older and younger than they: a blow
to their scriptural acumen? Their crabs have become
    shells—
while both Testaments know the virtue of crushing Stone.
(On the Confessional right, we find monastic cells;
though our gall returns, in suits of fine herringbone—
in wants. But God expects as much, sees us home;
we're white as Snow, in the '37 flick.
He puts us in place, just right for a lamb. We roam,
soft as Snow's chin, though her voice, is deeper, quicker
these days.) It's as He claims throughout this text.
He is the answer. Him. Nothing comes next.

Miserere
(MATTHEW 23:1–12)

We of the widened phylacteries, modest
engravings; these understated master threads
do please us! Counted moments—they're like white dress
at breakfast, while birds chorale! These days must be read
as the blessings they are, or, more completely, a wait
for heaven. This is all His doing, colored,
no doubt, with a tint of our presumption. It's the fate
we wait for, around the kitchen, cutlery; cullers
of a sort. We are not so different from you
or any man: schooling self-hate on a choke
chain. So when you see us, aloof, try a wider view.
(A boated refugee might need a smoke!)
Salvation only comes as a gift; it's news—
a pack of Luckies and a new friend. We can't lose.

The Sevenfold Indictment
(MATTHEW 23:13-32)

When our sins cut deeply, into our human need,
when they stampede like horses in our bloodstream,
when we rail near Innocents with our midnight screeds,
under a chaff of stars—His victory can seem
remote. My Down's son, for example, physically widens
to fill my need to console him. I would ease
his grief with treats—and so shorten his life. I chide
myself, as I help to spread the kindness disease.
And then there is vain-glory, another headstone
for my plot: to be read, loved, to find favor,
a need that runs so deep, most days, it could hone
the virtue humble discipline would savor.
I cannot wash my sins from my hands, says Maid
Macbeth. Let me fold my hands in unquiet shade.

The Untroubled Hand
(MATTHEW 23:33-39)

Why kill the wise ones? They never make any money,
grazing outside the pen. They're like sheep who call us
in their quiet — so who can hear? Their days are sunny;
they're dirt farmers, sincere. They put their trust
in what they cannot see. The truth never hides.
It's out in the fields. Prophets, like leaves that shake,
they could be crumbling buildings. You can confide
in them. (They only offer the things they make!
It's the mark they have to leave. That brings the trouble.
A word or a gesture, a blessing, a small public life —
this is because wisdom must move out. Love's double,
it offers the world a near-worthy sacrifice.)
The untroubled hand, once raised, defines its day.
You can find it on trains, in sky-scrapers, on bays.

70 AD
(MATTHEW 24:1-3)

Roman spears would crowd those hills, the rubble will
 thrum.
Jesus shows them specious glory, as what seems
can't be. The killing years, a tidy sum
has sealed the deal in white-washed praises. (Morning
 beams
can't save them — reject the King and your future ends.)
This temple's been spoken, now flesh becomes capstone —
His death will mean diaspora: sin rends.
Things can go no other way — their bones
will be scattered. Each shard will be forgotten, will sing.
(The hollower the gift, the more sure the fall.)
Had they druidic gardens, their history of wrong
might not seem so bad — some stone age Frodo's last call.
But close or far, each person has to repent.
Monuments can't help — once lives have been spent.

The Devil Ages
(MATTHEW 24:4-14)

Devils will have their day, though it's never clear
why. Perhaps it's because they've been created,
and are loved beyond any reckoning. (Like tears
on a face, what's pure must be pursued, dated.)
We'll hear Christ parodied, mouthed, as hell breeds
its wars. The earth will contract the ages, yawn open,
while God's gull steadies the air above us, frees
each open door—a capacity we hope in.
Only dread can soften His light. He cannot be shaken—
evil will sour nothing. The face of the devil
ages. His text offers no surprises. (His bacon's
been fried, a hundred times.) Only children know trills!
Every peaceful acre will know the cross's name,
every peat of gratitude. A sun will reign.

"Whoever Reads..."
(MATTHEW 24:15-25)

Matthew gets literary because Christ did, two times,
at least. How often have the Jews had to flee,
mad to the mountains? How many red suns would climb
the scaffold of morning, scarred moon, the bare trees
like skeletons, pregnant women skewered on swords.
How many pogroms were to come, impostures
leading countries. Few alive would be able to ford
those waters. (Each age must be burned, like old furniture.)
How repetitive each christ, til prayer make us new?
Surrounded by stench, a swarm of those lame voices
shorten our days, push heaven's hand. The spew
from Big Pharm — keeping people sick; these choices
thin us, as Satan's tabernacle* fouls the earth.
They can work their lies, offer smirks — but no mirth.

---

* Sr. Bridge McKenna's name for TV.

Wherever the Carcass Is
(MATTHEW 24:26–28)

The desert and inner rooms would be the most likely
places, which just means, don't follow your dread.
He won't be there. If you're anything like me,
He never comes in expected ways. We're fed
on mystery, the wholeness of Truth, pointed
in right directions. Lightning is the right word.
(He is the sky!) Vast, untrammelled, anointed
for this work; we'll see Him come in the habits of birds!
What have we ever understood? Certainly
not our lives — the carcass will be what's left of the world.
The most prized birds, eagles, feasting free!
Taut flags start to drop in the wind; big lies, unfurl.
We will wait for Him, much like we've always done,
or tried to do. We live, in a way, on the run.

The Last Symphony
(MATTHEW 24:29-31)

How still will it be? The last string of tribulation
will vibrate, begin to subside. The sun, blackened,
will be a coat no one can wear; homes done
with us. The moon will fissure, fail; it will crack
a porcelain in the sky. Then the greatest of signs:
Him; he'll begin, take hold, just before He descends.
What's human will moan, open the world—like a line
of fish on a river bank: the trumpets' blend.
People will feel his sandals in the sweat, the dust,
their feet; tall angels will walk with us as we gather
slowly, in winds, humble array. Our crust
will disappear, every small time hero, lather
in laughter. An oboe will reshape the sky.
Water will brim vases, shape pig and stye.

Even in Heaven
(MATTHEW 24:32-36)

Learn from the fig; its leaves come, and then summer, like
when your mate drew near. Who can know that touch,
that smile, that world before it happens — kids on bikes,
scenes created for each moment? So much
of this day is beyond us. That's why it's absurd to try
to hold on! Each end brings transition. God's Word
burns up April's green; each clipped lawn
is its declension. Creation is always spurred
by what must follow. Think of a rose's descent.
The gloam is His Word too, verb and verbiage,
forms of the passing Father. His impulse — spent
in virtuoso worlds, His speech, a storm
of passing creations. What must start is made to take us.
We'll know Him again, always pushing the limits of trust.

Late Test
(MATTHEW 24:37–44)

Let it not surprise you. You will be eating and drinking.
Not unpleasantly, or with rancor. The best, the bad,
the slightly askew. Others get taken, as you think
about some helping thing you might have said.
Your foolishness will be revealed to you,
still standing there, grinding at that mill
(which would be a good in itself: duty, the few
disciples still tending to their small corn stills).
Will you see souls arpeggio above you?
If so, that won't be the first time for that: Popes
and a Pio. You'll wonder as you shuck your corn — not blue,
but hopeful. Your life has taught you how to cope.
Nothing can matter, except for You, and Yours:
This weather is not new. It rains, it can pour.

In the Shack, Left Behind
(MATTHEW 24:45-51)

What matters grows in the servant's heart. How could
    things
be otherwise? The good, revealed as itself
must lie peaceably there, live what days bring.
(He seldom drinks out of season any more.) Less wealth
pulls at his older heart, though what seems virtuous
may just be wear, an unholy need to talk.
Stalks stand before him. His shed needs washing; he's just
an old man who drives his Chevy on grass! (His walking
stick makes for cool evenings.) He loves the people
he meets, though the small sample size does not help!
He bathes in the river at night, picks mushrooms. The
    steeple,
far-off bells remind him. Cur or whelp,
he waits behind. Others might come, of course.
All he has are his hands, a neighbor's fenced-in horse.

Irenaeus and Gnosis
(MATTHEW 25:1-13)

The wise harbor their quiet. But for wastrels who've
    toiled—
they question anything not their own. (Less stress
might be called for here if they held hands; the oil
for those who lead! Everyone placed. So much less
would be demanded of people, and God could enjoy
all our company.) That world, shared resources,
clean carbon footprints—a world for the hoi polloi.
"It takes a village, baby, different courses!"

But completion, the King, is Who we need to seek,
an us alongside. Hamlets halved can't be whole.
(Two rivulets must make a creek: we speak
both God and man, and a leaping story is told!)
Nothing else matters to saints—the face that forms them.
Our fingers find His cheeks; each leaf knows its stem.

God as a Mellon
(MATTHEW 25:14-30)

Is God a Rockefeller, reaping where
He hasn't sown, gathering where He's never
scattered seed? And then, more, does he want our spare
capital, to create more wealth which can only sever
us from the poor? Hasn't the Father ever read
the papers, seen Eva Perron's shoes, her closets?
Will we be judged by income, by those with the steady
eye of a jeweler who'll parse us and each bit
of our questionable lives? No. God just wants us to stand,
to become adults — heroes finally — to name
the virtue. He wants to walk next to us (no canned
laughter). He wants to smell our roses, the fame
we make. His head might be large for a game of hide
and seek, but think of those mesas, the breadth of
    each rise!

Lukewarm, or Just Middling
(MATTHEW 25:31–46)

What will it be like, after time, elbow to elbow,
next to near friends? It'll be dizzying, not a balm—
to be sorted! Maybe a pal, still in the throes
of his end, briefcase tucked; or the Ponytail palm
Jane carries. (She never really took to you
at work, and you never knew why!) Then our Lord and
    the weight
He brings, to the Mercy that carries us—we fed
our kids, a few guests, though not enough to rate
a badge. It's best to wait, regard the Man;
He dazzles, for the moment you get: soon, up close,
with your failings. Only He can save us, the wonderland
of our lives! (Who will have done enough?) For most
of my life—the parts that count—it's what He's done.
I'll walk beside the priests I've known, the nuns.

A One Man Show
(MATTHEW 26:1-5)

When Jesus pulled the curtain, the rings rattled,
closed above them, He sat on a bright-colored pillow,
baldly offered the cross. They twitched like spooked
    cattle—
fly-harassed ears, stopping mid chew, their lows:
an angst they could not yet feel. God stills suffers.
He knows the faintest of hearts—like when we sit
in pain, awaiting the end of our lives, each buffer,
friend, gone. We twist in earlier wishes, our snits
against the world.... Then Matthew pans to power.
Each bent hand plies, creates its will. For these,
there can be no peace, ever—no shade, no bower;
like empty cans, they implode, knuckle, on their knees.

Jesus slowly begins to take on their corruption, sin.
This is a one-man show. We have no in.

Beauty is Where It Finds You
(MATTHEW 26:6-13)

In a leprosarium, a woman loses
her way, pours fragrant oil over His hair—
perfect tension for an opening scene. (We must muse
to get the larger story: Matthew's "here.")
It's like Apparition Hill in Medjugorje.
You could be the crucial woman, oiling Matthew's
hair. One sits on rocky beauty; an apogee
of rosaries invite us to see Him through
the lies of this world. We're asked to stand in His stead
at Simon's house because that was for everyone.
The flask consumed wealth, the alabaster—the dead.
(The woman brought heaven, knowing His time was done.)
Some people hear this. They live where God is, slow
enough to wait for him to show. They grow.

A Man of Dice
(MATTHEW 26:14-16)

Thirty pieces of silver. They shine, no God, in the
    moonlight.
It's his last play to set things right: the world
rotted as they spoke: in flies, corpses! Things might
be turned. Rome wasn't the first drunkard to rise —
    each pearl
fractures, peels! How long must the remnant waste?
Must his own toothless mother scour for bread?
After all, Jesus acceded to every taste,
common man. With a turn of His smokey sovereign head
He could give reprise: ash for ash. (So Judas played
    outcomes.
He took up the prophetic, pedantic role. A man,
on the edge — every ounce of his bile given to feed
the slaughter. They were Jews! They would kill, stand
against time itself!) Each Messiah would do his part.
How else could they end this? How else could a rebirth
    start?

Miracles
(MATTHEW 26:17-19)

Small signs, created through Blake's particulars.
This time we get no tied-up donkey, colt.
Still, heaven is as graphic here as the stars
were on that Bethlehem night — as they were in a bolt
of cloth for St. Francis, or in Thomas Jefferson's
life, who disapproved, tried to cross them out.
Theologians, too, have squirmed to put life on the run.
Their world must not exceed reason's limits, be about
more than they know. Forget Carl Jung's dark grasp!
They have no time for Judas's dark suspicions,
for medieval burrs, rewards. They wanted a hasp
to close up their nothing. I'd rather dance with John's done.
Give me more myth than I can take, a world
where my life sits like a heavy tree, packed burls!

Clay Houses
(MATTHEW 26:20–25)

How does a blind disciple proceed? His wants
get worked out in models, perhaps, in clay houses,
the poses of miniatures on that street. Tiny Kant
walking timely past the buildings! A smaller mouse
or two watching him pass! Each new pose would offer
drama, an attitude about life. He might see
truth emerge. Though not the whole. He had to proffer
times, an angle, what type of biscuit, tea,
would serve the pathetic company — a small thing,
that town! (He would honor his because it honored
him.) He could see things clearly there: made a ring,
a key for Peter, a throne for John. (Connards!)
Each of their fingers, in his face, waving goodbye.
It would've been better for him . . . to invent a sty.

The First Tree
(MATTHEW 26:26–29)

The words invented our world: "This is my body."
That's how He creates, down to the crumbing bits
of dog-dug yard, scattered mulch, my shoddy
garage with its old jars of screws, the grit
that keeps our blood, neighborhood worship in order.
Altared, He becomes grain to eat, and more—
our road and deaths; and past cellular borders:
glucose, our heart sphincters. Ask Henry, his stores
of liquor. He's the Host who's opening volley rouses
the dogs of war. Let's be in tune. Let's be
our reach and demise. If we're present our small houses
can live there, behind that first impossible tree!
With this move, we're given life and a place on the altar.
It's a rowdy plan, makes the animal in us stir.

Peter's Pence
(MATTHEW 26:30-35)

Peter's got some bounce. He reminds us of young love's
first reach. Few characters in the Bible are so
unabashedly themselves. First in line, shovel
in hand, he powers away the garbage. He goes
to answers, always ready for the truth—not kind
and gentle like John, whose gaze could draw. He follows
to stand, like when he hacks off an ear (and finds
the end he's sought). He could be us, hollow
in our declarations—though he learns how to store
   the boast
when it deflates. ("Do you love Me?") We'd happily hoist
a few with recent Popes. They know that roast
of flesh. Each one's hung from humility's sacred joist.
Who wouldn't follow both men, now and then?
They master holes in the road—the turn of a wren.

Gethsemani
(MATTHEW 26:36-46)

When the weight of the world, a great millstone, drags you
under, when you're given no choice; your slipshod ways
define you. (It's a foul earthen spirit that drew
Him to His place, each ghost in the wind, a gray day.)
Plastic tears away from windows. (His time doesn't end—
the worst has begun!) A cur—like you, like me,
He knows our defeats. No one on earth can bend
or shape what has to happen. Like Him, we can see
our pain approaching—His death before it comes,
the citadel of heaven. He might be Anthony,
or the fish, gaping at his feet. The incessant drums
of God defeat us: His guts on a spoon, moonlit fees.
All of us must be raised, brought to the edges
of life—the shrieks among dark and stony hedges.

The Kiss
(MATTHEW 26:47–56)

Judas, flush with his hand, and help, had this:
a staged self. (This was the time to roar with lions!)
But Jesus, like His saints, was elsewhere, not blissed,
but in a larger Now. Not Judas's Zion—
but One that had to write us. (The self is a fine
potion, aromatic, like flowers in a morning breeze.
So it goes for all of us! We take a kindly
moment for more than a gift. We smile, say cheese,
and before you know it, we're face down again in the dirt,
meeting the Lord of our beginnings, our end.)
Jesus is always direct—our lives, like Mark's shirt,
put on, ripped off. Thank God our stylings rend
so easily. That's why our stages are small.
We'd block up history, the mirrors, the halls.

Can't Get There from Here
(MATTHEW 26:57-68)

Caiaphas, Peter open like new packs of cards,
while Popes, most often—anymore, away
from the action, move the quiet, like holy bards,
John of the Cross. This is how it is with each foray
into sin, each meister gets to play Attila:
"Are You the Son of God?" "Yes." (It never
seems to occur to them: Occam's flotilla—
He has to come to get here!) Being clever
has its drawbacks. Forever always seems to cut
into your now—like trees, inspiration. And since
they're not Jesus, they lash out: "Prophesy, Christ . . . what
hit You?" "The world . . . Just now it's insistence, rinsed."
The lost have their long screams for company.
When the music stops, they're surrounded by enemies.

The Best Sit Somewhere Else
(MATTHEW 26:69-75)

Peter's holy tears cannot absolve us.
Our cowardice is our own; that's why we sit,
coaxing fire to flames. The latest betrayal, the fust,
defining our souls. It's the weight of pomp, the tired bits
that bring the moon, goat gods to mind—our jive,
exposed, as the house girls have a smirk. "You're
    stream folk,
aren't you, the change to come?"...We're distant lives,
the other we hold out for, which seems a sordid joke.
The best sit somewhere else. We're branded, lies,
locked down, are stuck as we persist, still try
to fake our way—we're a set of false teeth that cries,
clattering along the ground. Let's watch the fly die!

But he's always been Peter, too, up-front, rough-hewn—
like some little kid, too many strings, balloons.

The Chief (and Lesser) Priests
(MATTHEW 27:1-2)

"A few more cow whippings and I can retire —
saved coins against the night. No more clandestine
candle-lit plans: the Tannin's two tails; each liar
forking the town in Dybbuk speech. (I'm the tin
that follows.) You'd think the clever would crow, hoot —
but they corner sooth-sayers at night; pre-eminence
must be wheedled, teased. They'd march in caligae, boots,
just to win the cry of the poor, that unruly, dense
necessity. God could come — not like this — and yet
who would hear Him, numbed by years of compliance,
taking the whips of our choosing, each imagined fete,
lauding our impact? (I watch the usual dance!)
I'd like to believe it could be: that God could live here.
But how would He find space, a big enough spear?"

Each Balanced Thing
(MATTHEW 27:3-10)

Judas elects his tragedy: "I have sinned,"
and his curtain hides him. ("And what was that to us?"
Empty hands are clean.) Like Cohen, Judas is pinned —
to the slight sound of protesting wings.... Then we cut
to the priests, above the fray; they consult, kneel
before process — the pages that protect them. Politicals
to the end (that won't come), they buy the potter's field.
They hide in corridors of codicils.
Judas, for his own reasons, ends the strife,
gives his life the cold closure he needs. Did the Lord
accept him? What makes repentance true, what knife
of ours can cut that deep? Only Jesus affords
that view. The span of His crucifixion rips
the world apart; each balanced thing must be tipped.

The King of the Jews
(MATTHEW 27:11-26)

Their disturbing laws interrupted her sleep. Her dreams
could not keep the peace what with insane high priests
dancing night blue around the fires — their schemes
running shops. They'd hang a prophet, account Him a beast
if that would help the till. (A messenger-angel
stood in arrears.) Her husband's hands iced in the bowl.
He was Rome's dog, she knew, so her cautionary knell
carried little weight. They were cogs — on a Roman dole.
"But what good could good possibly do? One had
to be ready to die for it, but even then,
why? To what end? These Jews deserved this mad
show. (They, too, had made the world a den
of filth, corruption.) She just wanted some comfort, ease:
a moment before the collapse, to create a cheese."

There is a Silence
(MATTHEW 27:27–31)

"A crown to top the scourged king. How much more blood
would this take? How much would make us foreigners
feel home? Since he was the Jew's king, we gathered mud
and dust to encase his life, a drop of myrrh!
We twisted the crown! Ripped off his robe. One more Jew,
like their God, ineffectual, who has no power
to challenge the reach of Rome! We marched past a few
of His women, past Jewish architecture — His bower.
Love has to be trampled like springtime flowers. The best
never see that coming. He died because he had to.
(We know we are not enough.) At the behest
of Caesar's daughter, death, we saw Him through.

Let it gall me. I need to see where, and who I am.
There is a silence that follows every lamb."

Then they Crucified Him
(MATTHEW 27:32-38)

Here we sit, in time, far away, on a Paris bench,
or in Weirton, with Eric Satie, playing piano
on Youtube. In front of the Crucified, we clench,
cast lots for our dress. (It's beauty that makes this so.)
"The King of the Jews" rules the bloodied few!
That would include us—two robbers on church walls.
We follow Him in the hilly mist, cool dew,
in a morning which invites strangers, as our world falls
into ruins. Did animals sin? What did dogs do?
Will they sit in obedient rows when He comes? Will
   flowers
open to receive His blood on their tongues? We stew
in our violence, even as we try to shower
our friends with our vacancies. Jesus came for them
as well—our quiet losses, our hidden gems.

The Louder We Talk
(MATTHEW 27:39-44)

Local idiots always wag their heads:
"Son of God, come down!" (Then they'd believe — but
   in what?)
And both robbers, too, try to relieve the dead.
(In Alphonse Liguori they seldom leave their ruts.)
They get the second last say. Jackals, made to fit,
or better, hyenas, with those laughs, those shortened
   back legs.
Too often we've sat among them, brandishing wit,
our sick need to belong. Such are the dregs
of approval, that almost created thing: the clamor
one makes to affirm oneself, audience of none;
we always seek it, this way or that, glamour,
the us we need. (We have a good day and we've won!)
The louder we talk, the less we have to say.
It's always so. It's how we ignore our days.

The Dead Out Walking
(MATTHEW 27:45-56)

Each created thing begins to lose cohesion,
slides us toward non-being; His unsaying voice —
as ours must become as we near our own deaths. (Reason
falls into place.) His last cry speaks His choice,
seals the temple's fate, as it rips, stops,
the dead, confused, who appear too early: Eastertide
right after Friday's host. Did their rising slop
in vacant alleys — while a quiet centurion slides
to his knees; we and the women, wanting Him back.
But life cannot rewind — no cosmic do-overs.
Time itself will follow that man, will track
him in his dust, as these women become his drovers
as they lead new disciples until the end of their days.
Their cries will dictate passage, how the new can stay.

Every Day under Sun
(MATTHEW 27:57-61)

As the evening closes in on itself, Joseph comes
with his lucre, puts it down (where he belongs),
while Pilate, misplaced soldier, tries to chum
with his dead through him, missing the campfires, songs:
a real life. Joseph moves on, in the silence of service;
he conducts servants through corridors of quiet.
They carefully wrap what's left in linen, nervous.
(They missed some of His teaching.) Joseph quells the riot
he feels inside, oversees sunken stone, his new tomb;
Magdalene (and that always other Mary)
sit outside, heads against rock, wait for the rooms
of morning, both feeling like they'd died or miscarried.
What did Joseph know of hope, how He binds one,
even before He arrives? Every day under sun.

A Pagan Pilate
(MATTHEW 27:62–66)

"The chief priests knew their rabble, too ignorant
to face the truth. They'd invent rapha, ghosts
if it kept them in a mysterious dark — a bent
band of 'chosens' with nothing but religious boasts
to buoy them. So my partners (in this crime) had to seal
their tombs, gave guards enough drink to keep the curious
away — a risen leader does have its appeal!
(That was all the city needed: a wraith, a spurious
king to usher in more dietary laws!)
I had to help them cut off the dog and pony
show, but the Jews pushed too hard, called back daws,
superstitions from an older vault. (Some free-
dom helps!) But their priestly lies will eat them alive.
They'll lose it all. What is pushed down revives."

"Your Sweet Wife/ Will Catch More Fish than You"
(MATTHEW 28:1-8)

The dawn's first light, realizing itself, quaked Mary
number one. A Taj Mahal* bird shot overhead;
another settled down in flowers, ripening berries.
They each saw the angel, thought their fishing-bed
was gone, as he danced on top, dime-spun the stone.
Then the angel grinned, sitting, bobbing musical legs.
His body laughed — then he did too. (The bones
of drunk guards rattled on cue.) "Come, see the dregs —
where He lay, then rise like bread and gather the guys
to catch some catfish supper along with the rhyme."
The first Mary yipped, jumped to snatch some sky.
Then they raced to catch His Galilean prime.
God is never where you think He is — catching fish
with bluesmen, under every star that makes its wish.

* American blues musician.

"Rejoice!"
(MATTHEW 28:9-10)

The Marys held His feet, would not let go.
They made some noises He didn't have to hear.
"Do not leave us." (He knew they needed Him to know.)
And in their silence, He gathered them in: their fears,
their love. "Do not fret. Just as one world ends,
the next begins." They would live to see the death
of their sin. He thought of Peter, smiled at the rending
he always insisted on. He remembered his breath,
the good will in each opinion — the smells, the sea.
And young John, he'd have the years to learn how to be.
So Jesus enjoyed the sand, which conformed beneath
his feet. He had to finish, to set everyone free.
We get some of that here, like when we rejoice at strangers,
or put our feet up — strawing a summer manger.

Our Elders
(MATTHEW 28:11-15)

The elders never finished, tried to cover His tracks.
How often He comes back! As we, working
through quieter versions of our sins, attack
our days, invoke His palimpsest, mercy. I clerk
in a little room, each notarized poem and hope
allowing Him to work, to move me, through labor,
toward heaven. Every good is His! Our limited scope
is the now—success is divinity's "yes," a favor.
Padre Pio knew this, though his life drove him up
an emotional wall. How great was his love, his need!
That's why he could play on the lawn, a persistent pup,
snorting, butt a-wag, insisting on some speed.
There's nothing he wouldn't do to set us free.
He might wait at a pingpong table, or on his knees.

The Riotous Good
(MATTHEW 28:16–20)

Some doubted the miraculous authority.
If you've ever put your head down, you probably
belong (sometimes) with these. But Jesus sees,
knows us. (That's why He invented climbing trees!)
So we praise God when we only hear soft wind
through bright or rainy boughs. It's all the same:
this sweetness. He follows us, like a corsage pinned
for a high school dance. Everyone is lame —
all those canes under cathedral glass. And still,
we must dance, since it's His love that has us here:
Jesus of naves, my daughter-lunches, the drill
in each retirement day. (And, of course, the beer.)
Jesus, let me push my stone; let no one see
or agree with the riotous good that captures me.

About the Author

DAVID CRAIG taught literature and creative writing at the Franciscan University of Steubenville for more than 30 years. These days he tries to sharpen what's left for him to do, serving his family, working poems, a novel. His wife, in the meantime, amid all of her interests (painting, sewing, classical piano), has surprisingly taken an interest in Stan Getz—whose music is currently playing in the kitchen.